FROM MANILA TO WALL STREET

FROM MANILA
TO WALL STREET

An Immigrant's Journey With America's First Black Tycoon

BUTCH MEILY

Heliotrope Books

New York

Heliotrope Books LLC
heliotropebooks@gmail.com

ISBN 978-1-956474-45-9 paperback
ISBN 978-1-956474-64-0 hardcover
ISBN 978-1-956474-44-2 eBook

Cover design by Cecile Aranez
Interior photos courtesy of Rene "Butch" S. Meily
Typeset by Naomi Rosenblatt with AJ&J Design

"As for man, his days are like grass, he flourishes like a flower of the field; The wind blows over it and it is gone, and its place remembers it no more."

—Psalm 103

This book is dedicated to my Mom and Dad who were always there for me, my son Marco who encouraged me to write it, my sisters Rose, Tess, Finina, and Susan and my brother Jim, and to good old God for His many blessings. *Ad Majorem Dei Gloriam.*

FOREWORD

My beloved husband, Reginald F. Lewis, was a larger-than-life figure who influenced the lives of everyone around him, like a hurricane or an earthquake.

I told the story of my life with him in my autobiography, *Why Should Guys Have All the Fun?* (John Wiley & Sons, Inc. 2023). It is Part 2 because his biography *Why Should White Guys Have All the Fun?* is Part 1 (John Wiley & Sons, Inc 1995).

However, Reg was a complicated man with many sides to his personality. Butch Meily, who served as his public relations adviser, often saw a side of Reg I glimpsed only from time to time. *From Manila to Wall Street* brings Reginald back to life and unveils a portrait of Reg that is as deep and insightful as any to date. At Reg's side during many of the pivotal events in his career, including his acquisition of TLC Beatrice International, Butch describes Reg's brilliance, his strategic acumen and his staunch determination to break new barriers in the white business world and dispel the lie that Black people are not as capable as everyone else.

Butch was the quintessential "inside man" at TLC Beatrice as, with Reg, he played in the high stakes corporate game of the 1980s and 1990s, achieving prestige and success beyond his wildest dreams.

In the book, too, Butch goes beyond that stunning success story by telling the tale of his own life as a Filipino immigrant in America—like me—who, first on his own and then through his work with Reg, made the American Dream come true.

Today, Butch helps victims of calamities in his work for the Philippine Disaster Resilience Foundation. Although his story with Reg ended decades ago, Butch's own story continues.

Loida Nicolas Lewis
New York City
May 2024

AUTHOR'S NOTE

From 1987 to 1993, as pioneering African American entrepreneur Reginald Lewis achieved the biggest business successes of his career, I was there. I joined him during those six intoxicating years in many of the events before and after the billion-dollar acquisition of Beatrice International that defined his legendary career, and in much else besides. I was in corporate boardrooms, private homes, and luxury resorts in New York, Paris, the Hamptons, Cap' du Antibes in the south of France, and St. Moritz. I flew the supersonic, ultra-chic Concorde and Beatrice's private plane. And the entire experience was one of the great adventures of my life. In *From Manila to Wall Street*, I tell this story in detail.

Nevertheless, some events occurred that shaped his mission and our work together at which I was not present. For example, I did not attend certain meetings and discussions related to the Beatrice bid, auction and closing. To omit those episodes from this book would leave key gaps in my story of the period of our work together and how I came to have the opportunities with him that I did. Accordingly, in writing this work, I have reconstructed and, in some cases, imagined those episodes based on various sources. These sources include my recollections of my conversations with Reginald Lewis himself at or around the time those events occurred, interviews with key participants in those events, the 1995 biography of Reginald Lewis entitled *Why Should White Guys Have All the Fun?* by Blair Walker (John Wiley & Sons, 1995) and my understanding of the personalities involved. Where other accounts of events differ from my recollections, especially when describing events at which I was present, I have relied on and prioritized my recollections.

In addition, in several parts of the book, I combined various discrete scenes into one for dramatic purposes, and I have taken the liberty of inventing a couple of scenes that I think realistically portray Reginald Lewis as the person I knew him to be. As a result, those scenes are not meant to be a historical record of events but more of a stylized portrayal of a combination of various conversations and impressions folded into one setting. A list of the events or scenes that I have reconstructed, combined, or created, and the sources used for those events and scenes, appears in the Scene List at the end of the book.

My hope is that the book will shine a light on a particular time and place from the last century and the people who played key roles in that drama. Reginald Lewis changed my life and that of countless others. May his story and mine including our pursuit of the American Dream and my subsequent life as a humanitarian inspire people of all races and backgrounds for generations to come.

PROLOGUE

I have made a living by attaching myself to powerful people and found it to be a profitable pursuit. My ex-mother-in-law says I'm lucky that way. I'd like to think that they found me to be honest, non-judgmental, close-mouthed about their secrets and basically a nice guy, but my former wife might disagree. Nevertheless, I made a career of these alliances without even realizing it at the time. Maybe it was just convenient. But they all trusted me, some more than others. That connection, however, has cost me perhaps what I most wanted in life: love, a family, a home. If I'd had the gift for prophecy, I might have made different decisions. But looking back, decisions and events seem to have followed one upon the other, preordained and bound together like one ship pulled by another. I was both participant and observer in these comings and goings, possessing this curious self-awareness and the ability to take myself out of a scene and watch it unfold around me.

There was the Jamaican Prime Minister, the PR maniac, the Asian tycoon. But it is Reginald Lewis's story—the businessman who successfully bid a billion dollars for Beatrice International, a corporation made up of 64 companies in 31 countries and became the richest African American of the time, only to die at the age of 50—that I most need to tell before my memory fades. One of his French executives compared him to the sun, around whom all of us minor planets revolved. He haunts me still.

Now that I'm on the slippery, downward slope of life, I have finally found the words to tell that story and my own which are bound together and decided to write it all down, come what may, as both a cautionary tale and an act of remembrance.

1 – "CALL ME 'REG'"

It was the 1980s, the decade of Ronald Reagan and deregulation, of Cyndi Lauper and Michael Jackson, of extravagance and excess, where getting rich was on everyone's mind. New York had been in a long period of decline and people were desperate to escape it. But for an immigrant kid from the Philippines, the city held an attraction that has never faded. It felt like a slap in the face, waking me up from years of torpor. Here, I single-mindedly pursued my ambitions, unfettered by prejudice or entanglements of any kind. I'd scaled the public relations ladder, jumping from one firm to the other, until I finally landed a job with Burson Marsteller at the age of 32, the "Harvard" of PR firms. It was a global behemoth with annual revenues at one point of over $200 million and thousands of employees and offices around the world.

In those days, big American companies were being taken over by people we'd never heard of through leveraged buyouts, commonly called LBOs[1]. LBOs made use of "other people's money," money that was borrowed, to acquire a corporation by using the assets of that same corporation as collateral for the loans. It was like someone using the rope that you made and sold to hang you. Many of these LBOs were backed by one investment bank that the rest of Wall Street despised: Drexel Burnham Lambert. Just hearing their name struck fear in the hearts of every executive in corporate America and the revolution was led by one man, Michael Milken.

At Burson, I joined the mergers and acquisitions PR team, where we devised strategies to place positive stories, spread negative news, hold employee rallies, take out full-page ads, and use all kinds of publicity to benefit our clients' causes. We were either on offense or defense. It didn't matter to us as long as we got paid.

---

[1] A leveraged buyout or LBO is a financial transaction to acquire a company which takes on a considerable amount of debt and often uses the assets of that company as collateral for the debt.

These were knock-down, take-no-prisoners affairs and only one side would get to keep their jobs at the end. Corporate executives, who were under siege, realized that what was at stake were not just their company-paid country club memberships, their kids' private school educations, and their heavily mortgaged mansions, but also their very sense of who they were, their place in society. If they lost these takeover battles, all that would be gone.

One summer day in July 1987, I was sitting in my windowless, sparsely decorated cubicle in the Burson office on East 19th Street and Park Avenue South, pretending to work hard when the phone rang. A woman was on the line, and she said her name was Loida Lewis. She called me Butch, a childhood nickname that my parents gave me after a *Saturday Evening Post* cartoon about an overweight burglar with a mask. I guess they had a sense of humor because I don't know too many parents who name their kids after burglars. She said she'd gotten my name from a *Wall Street Journal* reporter and from her accent, I could tell she was a "kababayan," a fellow Filipino.

"My husband has a PR problem," she said. "Don't worry. He'll be a big client someday." She told me someone would call and hung up.

I spoke to my boss Chris Atkins about it. Chris was just a little older than me, but he'd already written a book about PR, a copy of which I'd asked him to autograph. He wore a neatly cut head of brown hair and had a clear, direct gaze. He never seemed to get too excited except when the market crashed later that year and he abruptly broke off a meeting to tell me he had to bail out of the market "for my own account." After we talked, Chris told me to go for it.

The phone rang again, and it was someone who told me his name was Everett Grant and that he worked for Reginald Lewis, the CEO of TLC Group and that they did leveraged buyouts. I had no idea who Reginald Lewis or TLC Group was. There were no Google searches back then. But he proceeded to interview me, and then, evidently satisfied with my answers, put me through to the man himself.

A deep voice came on the line. "I'm Reginald Lewis. Call me Reg." And that's how I came into contact with the most extraordinary person I've ever met.

Reg proceeded to tell me his problem. He'd recently sold McCall, an old-line sewing pattern company, but in *The New York Times'* story about the sale, the new British owners and the managers never acknowledged the work he'd done turning the company around and improving profits. So, Reg, being the kind of guy he was, looked up the reporter's number in the phone book—

which was something you could do in those days—and woke him up at six in the morning to yell at him.

The reporter's name was Dan Cuff and I happened to know him. Accordingly, I reassured him, "Don't worry, Reg; I know the guy. I'll set up an interview for you and we'll get the problem fixed."

My goal was to get Cuff to write a second story on the McCall sale, one based on a meeting with Reg where he'd get a chance to give Cuff his side of the story. I called Cuff, who was understandably incensed. I tried to calm him down.

"Who does that guy think he is? I've never had anyone do that to me before."

"Take it easy, Dan. He's actually a good person. He just feels like he got a raw deal." I arranged to have Reg and I meet him at his office at the *Times* so that we could explain things and perhaps even coax a second, more positive story about McCall from him.

That night, I clambered down to my rundown studio apartment with pipes cutting across the ceiling on First Avenue and 73rd street on what was known as the Upper East Side. My landlord had described it to me as a garden apartment because you could see a slice of grass and pavement through a window running along the top of one side. Cute lamps stood next to a well-worn, cheap couch set against the wall, which faced the all-important 36-inch TV. A plaque labeled "How To Be A Success" filled with colorful illustrations and caricatures on how to do just that—"Organize a Plan," "Maintain a Positive Attitude"—that I'd bought from a Central Park vendor hung on the wall. A folding curtain made of capiz shells (a form of oyster) imported from the Philippines separated a bed from the rest of the apartment. Coming out to meet me with a glass of white wine in her hand was a slim Filipina, ten years younger than me, light-complexioned with brown hair. She was dressed in a flowing white blouse and pants, had medium-length hair and wore hardly any make up. She had a big smile on her face as if she'd been waiting for me all day, hugged me and planted a kiss.

Her name was Pam, short for Pamela, my girlfriend. It was still the early days of our living together, but we had already begun to fall into this 1950s ideal of a male-female relationship, where I focused on my career while she took care of things at home, even though she had a degree from Pratt and a job as a junior interior designer. It was a paradigm that we'd inherited from our parents and that I felt to be natural and comfortable. It didn't matter what time of day it was, Pam was always made up and well dressed, a lady down to her fingertips. She even kept pictures of Audrey Hepburn in the closet to remind her of what class and style meant.

I told her about the Reg Lewis call and said that although I was excited and saw it as an opportunity, I knew next to nothing about him.

"What do you have to lose?" she said. "This could mean new business that you'd bring in for Burson and that can't hurt. Butch, you're good with the press."

I was relatively new at Burson and, aside from a trip to Spain to defend a sugar company against a hostile takeover by the Kuwaiti Investment Office, I felt that I hadn't accomplished much. Pam had a way of reassuring me that was enormously important. Although she was younger, she was more street smart than I was, buried as I was in my books and movies. Pam was my best friend, my confidante. I felt that I could ask her anything and couldn't wait to tell her stories about my day. And I loved her.

The next afternoon, I waited patiently in the lobby of the *Times* when in strode through the revolving doors a short, husky man with a moustache and close-cropped dark hair. He conveyed a brooding presence and purposeful-ness, and he was good looking in a rough sort of way. But what drew attention to him was an intensity, a drive, a feeling of caged energy ready to spring.

It wasn't till he walked through those doors that I realized he was Black. I was surprised because in those days, there weren't too many African Ameri-cans in the New York business world.

He looked me right in the eye, reached out his hand, and said, "I'm Reg Lewis."

His hand was clammy when I accepted it in a shake and beads of sweat formed on his forehead. I did my best to calm him down. Later, I learned that he harbored a deep distrust for the white mainstream press, viewing them as racist. I started briefing him about the interview, even though we'd already discussed it in detail on the phone a few times.

"Any last words of advice before we go up?" he asked.

I tried to think. I sensed that I needed to share something to shore up his confidence.

"Just be yourself. You've got a great story. You'll be fine," I told him and with that, we hopped on the elevator. It was a rare thing to be allowed entry into the inner sanctum of what was known as The Gray Lady. I think it was my first time inside and I felt the majesty and sacredness of it sweep over me as I entered the cathedral. Rows of reporters in ties and rolled up shirtsleeves banged away at their desktop computers. There was a continuous, noisy buzz hanging over the newsroom, which seemed to stretch on forever.

Cuff was a mild-mannered, white-haired, middle-aged guy who welcomed us at his desk. He pulled out his notebook and waited. Reg began to tell his story, taking us through the three years of hard work that he and TLC Group[2] put into the company. Cuff scribbled furiously.

"When I bought McCall—"

"That was a leveraged buyout, right?"

"Yes, it was. I bought the company for $22.5 million."

"Of mostly borrowed money?"

"That's how leveraged buyouts work," Reg said as he began to tap his fingers rat-a-tat-tat on Cuff's desk. "McCall was an old-fashioned home sewing pattern company when I took over. I opened up new sources of revenue, like greeting cards, that no one had ever thought of. Can you believe that? A sewing pattern company that turns out Valentine's Day cards! The old-time managers were amazed. Profits jumped."

Reg warmed up and he began to use his hands like instruments, drawing us in. He flashed a boyish grin of pride at what he had accomplished. A radiant energy swept out from him and caught both Dan and me in its wake. I could tell that after an initial hesitation and coolness, Dan had fallen under his spell. I did my bit to keep the conversation going, but for the most part, it was Reg's show.

The meeting ended almost two hours later, and Dan walked us to the elevator. I promised to send him a photo of Reg in case he could use it. As we exited the *Times*, Reg offered me a ride in his chauffeur-driven blue Bentley. Once inside, he asked me how I thought the interview went. Just getting him the interview with Cuff was a PR coup. I was ebullient. I knew that I'd scored a home run.

Or so I believed.

"I thought it went really well. You and Cuff had a rapport, which is import-

___

[2] TLC stood for The Lewis Company. At the time, what the initials stood for was a closely guarded secret. TLC Group was the vehicle for Reginald Lewis' leveraged buyouts.

ant if we want to get a positive article out of this."

All of a sudden, his smile vanished, his tone changed, and all his nervous energy suddenly unleashed itself on . . . me. "Well, I fucking didn't! He was pretty ignorant for a goddamn *New York Times* business reporter. You noticed how he sneered at LBOs?"

"He didn't sneer at LBOs." I was not prepared to go along with his version of the interview and I felt compelled to defend the decent human being who'd given us a second chance.

"How do we know what that cocksucker is going to write?"

I was stunned. "I'll be feeding him material for the story."

"You'd better stay on top of this one, Butch. The message is a ninety-to-one return for my investors. That's critical for a new deal that I'm working on. There's got to be no mention in the story about my being Black. This isn't a 'Black' business success. It's an American business success. But just to let people know that I am Black, we need a photo. You've got to get the photo in the story. That'll be enough." He tugged at his tie. Gobs of spittle formed on his lips. He almost seemed to burst from his seat.

The harangue went on until, at last, I asked if I could get out and walk. I had just seen a different Reg Lewis, not the smiling fellow who I'd gone up in the elevator with just a short time ago. I staggered out of the car and on to the city streets. I had just met this guy and already he was yelling at me. The only words that I hadn't heard were "thank you."

Three nights later at 10:30, I trudged through the streets of Manhattan looking for a newsstand. Back then, you could get a copy of the next day's paper if you stayed out late enough. I couldn't sleep without catching a glimpse of the story and its contents. To get everything Reg wanted, especially the picture, into *The New York Times* would be unbelievable, if not impossible. But I'd been working hard with Cuff on the article. Finally, I spied a place in Midtown that was open. I had to tell myself to calm down as I bought a copy of the paper and flipped to the business section. I told myself not to expect too much.

Then I saw it. On page 3 of the business section, below the fold, was a story headlined "90-to-One Return for Investors" and a photo of a fierce-looking, mustachioed Black man. The opening lines of the article read:

Reginald F. Lewis's first leveraged buyout was for a relatively small company, but it was a huge success. He cashed out with a 90-to-1 return...'This kind of return puts you in the top, top upper levels. He is a very creative financial person… Unlike some financial people, Mr. Lewis rolled up his sleeves and got involved in the direction of his company,' said an investment banker from First Boston, one of the sources that I'd provided Cuff.

The article continued: *Mr. Lewis, 44, is an intense lawyer who is likely to call an associate at 6 a.m. to deal with a problem,* a little backhanded slap from Cuff about his first encounter with Reg. Then more about his background. *He was born in Baltimore and went to Virginia State University and the Harvard Law School. He came to New York and joined the corporate law department of Paul, Weiss, Rifkind, Wharton & Garrison until the early 1970's when he left to co-found a law firm, Lewis & Clarkson. He has been a director of the New York City Off-Track Betting Corporation.*

I could hardly believe my eyes. I had done it! I ran to the nearest phone booth and, trembling a little, dialed Reg's home number. A woman answered. It was Loida.

"Loida, can I talk to Reg, please? It's important."

To my surprise, she declined. "No, I'm sorry, Butch. He's already sleeping and I can't disturb him."

"But I've got great news," I insisted. "I have tomorrow's *New York Times* story and it's a good one. I need to tell him about it."

"No, I'm sorry. He needs his rest. I'll tell him tomorrow when he gets up."

I could not believe it. I'd roamed the streets of the city to get a copy of the best story I'd ever placed, and my client who'd been pressuring me for the last four days was sound asleep.

"All right. Please tell him I called and that the article has everything he wanted. It's an exceptional story," I said dejectedly.

And it was. The *Times'* piece turned Reg into a minor celebrity in Wall Street circles. I had no idea then what the article would lead to, or the change and upheaval it would bring into my life. Placing it in the *Times* was important for my career but I found out later that this single news story would help carry Reg within reach of his big moment.

Reg was a tough customer. But I had met other tough men in my life before. One of them was my father.

2 – THE BEGINNING, 1977

My father, Joe Meily, grew up in Manila under the American flag and recited the Pledge of Allegiance in school. The Philippines had been a U.S. colony for almost fifty years after being under Spanish rule for almost 400 and had just gained its independence in 1946. The old joke was that we'd spent 400 years in a convent and fifty in Hollywood.

During the Second World War, the Japanese bombed airfields in the Philippines just ten hours after they'd attacked Pearl Harbor on December 7, 1941. Their invasion force swept through the country, only getting held up for months by strong resistance from American and Filipino forces in a last ditch fight at the Bataan peninsula and Corregidor island. Those soldiers finally surrendered on April 9, 1942.

By early 1945, the Americans had returned with a vengeance and with the support of Filipino guerrillas had reconquered much of the country with the exception of Manila and scattered outposts. In Manila, a Japanese Navy contingent, against orders, resolved to fight to the end. They murdered everyone they could find as the American Army approached the Philippine capital. Over 100,000 civilians died in the old city during the fighting. My mother, Annie, told me stories of her friends being lined up in schools and churches for what they thought would be a routine roll call, only to be bayonetted or shot by the soldiers. She and her family were only able to escape because a Japanese neighbor warned them to leave Manila because things were going to get bad as the Americans got closer. These tales intrigued me because they conjured up a world that was so different from mine, with bayonets and murder and soldiers battling in old Manila's cramped streets.

Joe was called up as an ROTC graduate just before the war began, became a second lieutenant, and was captured at Bataan when American and Filipino forces surrendered to the Japanese. He survived the 65-mile-long Death

March under a blazing hot April sun and more than a year at a prisoner-of-war camp. Somewhere from 5,000 to 18,000 American and Filipino prisoners died during the Death March.

Before the war, Dad had seen the baseball gods Babe Ruth and Lou Gehrig hit home runs at the old Rizal Memorial Baseball Stadium in Manila as part of a tour of Asia by an All-Star team. He and I stayed up late at night so we could listen on the Armed Forces Radio Service as the St. Louis Cardinals won the World Series in 1964 and 1967.

"Hijo (Spanish for son, which is what older people called their kids back then), Bob Gibson is pitching a tremendous game."

"Yes Dad," I answered sleepily. "But I like it better when there are a lot of home runs."

"Hijo, you have to see pitching as a battle between the pitcher and the batter. One man against another. And then you'll see how exciting this part of the game really is," he said as he fiddled around with the radio set.

Joe left a cushy advertising job at a large corporation in Manila to start his own marketing firm and my mother, who'd topped the national exams for Pharmacy, became his workmate, helping keep track of things. He quit the corporate life because he couldn't stand having to stay at the office until 9 p.m. every night or until whenever the boss felt like going home. I thought we might have had more money if he'd stayed at his job, but I felt proud of him for having the courage to strike out on his own. On the side, he and my mother devoted years to writing a husband-and-wife advice column on marriage and family life in a national magazine. They gave talks all over the country and pioneered in the profession of counselling troubled couples. It became a common sight at home to see glum-looking men and women waiting anxiously to confer with my parents. I told myself I'd never end up like those people. My parents had even written a couple of well-received books on marital issues. I looked up to them enormously.

I was born in Manila on December 21, the shortest night of the year and the winter solstice—although I'm not sure what that means in a tropical climate—in the middle of the 20th century. I'd grown up watching old Hollywood movies on TV or American shows like *Star Trek* or *Combat*. Every afternoon after school ended, I hurried home to catch whatever was showing on our black-and-white TV, which was a luxury in those days. There'd always be some war picture or a musical. I especially liked Jimmy Stewart and Gregory Peck.

My boyhood had been relatively strict at the Ateneo, a Jesuit school run back then by mostly American Jesuits. In grade school, we wore uniforms and shuffled to Mass every Friday. We had rosary checks by old Fr. Pollock, half blind and in a wheelchair.

"All right, boys! Let's see your rosaries," Fr. Pollock would tell us. Then each of us would have to file past him to show him our rosaries.

I tried to avoid him for confession because his penances were severe. Five Our Fathers and five Hail Marys at a minimum and an entire rosary for really bad offenses.

"You did what? During Holy Week of all times!" Fr. Pollock would lecture me at confession.

We drew a cross and the motto, "AMDG," the Latin expression "Ad Majorem Dei Gloriam," for the greater glory of God, the Jesuit motto, at the top of every paper we wrote or homework that we turned in.

One female teacher made me eat paper for talking during class.

"Meily, Ilagan, I told you to stop talking," Mrs. Palma yelled at us. "Pull out a piece of pad paper. Crumple it and start chewing."

Perhaps it might have tasted better with Worcestershire sauce. She ordered my seatmate, George Ilagan, to sit in front of the class in a corner for a second offense.

High school was different. It opened up new worlds of literature, debating, and sports to me. Our English teachers like Ernest Belamide, Ralph Cecilio, Rudy Dula, and Wally Yerro were passionate about learning and introduced us to many wonderful stories and writers like Hemingway and Steinbeck. But it too had its rules. I often had to stand "post" for an hour for being late to class. That meant standing at attention in a hallway while everyone giggled and sneaked around you. Often, I was forced to write what we called a jug.

"Meily, you're late again! Go ahead and write a jug," said Pol Mata, our resident disciplinarian and sadist. "Write, I will not be late for class 200 times. The next time you're late, I'm going to make it 1,000 times."

This happened so frequently that I developed a callus on my finger. The strange thing was that I lived just a few blocks from the school. I occasionally biked to class with my brother Jim holding on to me. The exchange for all that was what my professors at the University of Florida later called "obviously an education of the highest quality." And the lesson that it was better to be a good loser and "cheer as the winners walk by" than to win unfairly.

By the late '60s and '70s, the Philippines like the rest of the world was changing. Drugs cut a swath through our school. Friends died of overdoses. A wave of Communist instigation and propaganda flooded the country, fueled by the Vietnam war where the Philippines deployed engineering battalions to support the American war effort. Crowds sang the Filipino version of the Communist anthem, "L' Internationale," in the streets.

My college years were chaotic. Martial Law was proclaimed in 1972 during our sophomore year and, unless you were part of the ruling clique or knew someone who was, life was a dead end. A nightly curfew was enforced by soldiers deployed at checkpoints and they didn't hesitate to shoot if you didn't stop. The declaration by President Ferdinand Marcos came just months before the end of his second and final term in office. It seemed like a ploy for him to stay in power longer.

At first, Martial Law appeared to be a way to change the country and improve people's lives, but it morphed into a thuggish dictatorship where the president's cronies stole control of corporations and public funds, turning themselves into mega millionaires overnight. The almost-daily demonstrations and boycotts—no class!—ended and a blanket of silence punctuated by a relentless drumbeat of good news, martial anthems and calls for discipline fell over the land. Every now and then, whispered reports of people disappearing in the middle of the night reached us. All of the opposition politicians were in jail or had fled to the relative safety of nearby U.S. Air Force and Naval bases.

Soon after Martial Law was declared, many of the kids who were older than me ran off to the hills to join the rebel group that was fighting the government. Soldiers killed our college student council president and the head of our debating society in encounters on far-off islands. The day Martial Law was declared, a classmate hurried over to the house and handed me some documents to hide.

"Just hold them for me for a couple of days," he urged me. I wasn't in the movement, but I agreed to do it for friendship's sake. I stuck them under a bin in the garage. The next morning, he was picked up by the military. When his brother had the impertinence to confront the officer in charge and demand his release, his body turned up the next day floating in a river, his head bashed in. Apparently, the officer didn't like something he said.

After I graduated, inspired by my father's advertising career, I landed a job in public relations at one of the country's largest corporations, San Miguel. But I saw no future for me under Martial Law and like so many other Filipinos, I cast my eyes overseas. So one humid July day in 1977, I bid goodbye to my parents and my brother and four sisters at the old Manila airport. I was heading for Gainesville, Florida, a place I'd never heard of and had a hard time picking out on a map, to get a Master's degree in Journalism and Communications from the University of Florida. Thanks to my job in corporate PR, I'd bagged a scholarship that came with a part-time job as a graduate assistant. I was 23.

At the airport, crowds of Filipinos indulged in our age-old custom of flocking to the airport to see people off, crying, waving, and shouting at them. Then everyone would dine at an upstairs lounge with large windows overlooking the tarmac and watch the planes take off. That airport later mysteriously burned down in the middle of the night after an exposé appeared in a local paper about customs and other anomalies there.

I prepared to board the plane and leave the city for the long trip to the States which was a big deal back then. Except for a brief trip to Hong Kong, which was still a British colony, I'd never been abroad. I had no idea what to expect. I only knew America from the movies and TV I watched and the books and magazines I read like *Time, Newsweek, Life,* and *Reader's Digest.* I had two uncles who were American GIs who'd stayed behind after the war and married my Dad's sisters. I was close to some of the American Jesuits who'd taught me. In those days, the Philippines was part of the New York province of the Jesuit order; so they all came from Brooklyn, the Bronx or Queens to teach and live the rest of their lives among us. Men like Dick Croghan, Charlie Duffy, Doug Kull, Bill Kreutz, Chris Conroy, Pat Murphy, Patrick Lynch and Pat Giordano. They were track, softball and debating coaches. English, chemistry, theology and speech teachers. One or two of them shared a love for San Miguel Beer with me. Many eventually left the Jesuits. But I felt a deep kinship and fondness for them. That was the sum total of what I knew about America. I admired it, at least from afar.

My family hovered around me. I was the eldest child and very close to my parents. My mother hugged me as she predicted, "Butch, you're going to like it there so much, you won't want to come home."

"Don't worry, Mom. I'll be back. But I've got to go. There's nothing for me here."

My father pulled me aside and handed me $1,000. At first, I resisted, but he forced me to accept it. The cash was a big deal to me because I was heading off without a whole lot in my pocket.

"Take this. You'll need it, hijo. You're going to be on your own. But I've always believed that the most valuable present that I could give you is a good education. As long as you have that, you'll be fine."

"I know, Dad. I'm grateful. I'll be all right."

"The U.S. is a great and fascinating land and people, especially the people, and you'll feel that as soon as you step on their soil. They have tremendous strengths and good qualities; but, being human, they also have their weaknesses, and these can be contaminating. You haven't given your mother and I anything but honors that make us proud and full of joy for having a son like you in this cruel day and age."

He put his arm around me.

"It breaks my heart to see you go," my father said. "But you'll be living the life that I've always dreamed of. Remember us and pray for us always and we'll be with you wherever you may be."

I began to pull away.

"One last thing: always stay close to God and you can't fail."

I wanted to linger with my family a bit longer. But my younger brother, Jim, who was still in school and who I yelled at a lot, was eager to finally get his own room (the happiest day of his life, he later told me) and egged me on.

"You'd better go. You might miss the plane," he chided.

With that encouragement, I picked up my few possessions and walked toward the aircraft, stopping just long enough to take one last look at those who were dearest to me in all the world and mouth a silent, "I love you."

I had no idea then just how far or how high that flight would take me.

3 – THE DEAL, 1987

Reg showered me with rare praise over *The New York Times* story. I made a glossy copy of the article and had it framed for him. I kept another copy of it above my desk at the office. I'd scored a hit, which is what we called it when we placed an article or a radio or TV interview. Media relations was one of my specialties in the PR field and it felt good to get a piece in the *Times*.

Reg promptly hired Burson and I was put in charge of the account. Finally, I'd brought in some business for the firm. I felt like I belonged because I wasn't just servicing an account. Reg Lewis and his firm, TLC Group, were all mine. It was in a new field too that was just opening up as the next frontier for PR firms, mergers and acquisitions, leveraged buyouts. At first, we all thought it was going to be a small piece of business. And for a month, it was. Then one night in August 1987, just a month after the *Times* article, the phone rang. It was Reg. He asked me to come over to his place. I wasn't sure what the reason for the rush was but my heart beat a little faster when I got his summons. It was late. I took a cab to his apartment in Chelsea, East 21st Street and made a mental note to add that to my expenses. I ran up the steps and rang the bell. He opened the door and gave me a huge smile. He was still in his office clothes minus the coat and tie. I could tell he was excited about something. He asked me in, and I made myself comfortable on a couch in the living room of the two-story brownstone. There was a fireplace on one side and a side table with a large TV on it. The toys of his two young girls lay draped on the chairs. He started talking animatedly.

"I wanted to bring you in on this early. That article of yours at the *Times* really hit the spot. I got a call to come to LA and meet this guy who I'd talked to about the McCall deal, but it didn't work out. His name is Mike Milken. Ever heard of him?"

"Of course. Who hasn't? He and Drexel are doing all these big corporate takeovers."

Milken was like the godfather of a rambunctious portion of Wall Street.

He'd unleashed a revolution by harnessing the power of high yield bonds, also known as junk bonds,[3] to drive takeovers of huge corporations. RJR Nabisco, Revlon, Safeway supermarkets, TWA airlines—they would all fall to the takeover craze with their staid corporate managers getting tossed out in favor of new owners with unfamiliar names but big personalities like Ron Perelman, Carl Icahn, Irwin Jacobs, T. Boone Pickens.

Previously, company executives had taken pride in having little to no debt on their balance sheets. But in the 1980s, under the more relaxed attitude of President Reagan, debt began to be seen as smart. Through junk bonds, Milken created an innovative way for financiers to borrow more money and to use it to buy up corporations, break them up and sell the pieces, earning huge amounts of money in these transactions.

Reg told me about his fantastic plan. He was not a man who dreamed small. "There's this company, Beatrice. It has all the brands: Tropicana orange juice, Samsonite luggage, Avis. But it also has this huge overseas business, Beatrice International. Sixty-four companies in 31 countries! Can you believe it? All food companies, most of them market leaders. There's going to be an auction for Beatrice International and I plan to bid for it with Milken's help." He practically choked on his words in his excitement. "KKR bought the whole thing a year ago, remember? For $8.7 billion."

I remembered. It was one of the biggest business stories of the time, a traditional, well-known conglomerate wolfed up by Kohlberg, Kravis & Roberts, KKR. KKR topped the list of what later came to be known as "the barbarians at the gate." They used Milken and his junk bonds to fund hostile takeovers of many of the companies that made up the heart of corporate America. Together, they flipped the business world upside down, throwing out the longtime, entitled corporate managers and replacing them with a new crowd. They overturned the social pyramid as well. The magic of junk bonds transformed people who were once nobodies into kings and barons of society. And this was the social class that Reg longed with all his heart to join.

KKR had bought Beatrice in 1986 in what at the time was the largest leveraged buyout in history. It then proceeded to sell off its assets to repay the debt it had incurred in the purchase. One of those assets was Beatrice's

---

[3] High yield or junk bonds are financial instruments that corporations who have a low credit rating issue at higher interest rates to attract investors. They are seen as speculative or high risk because these corporations can default or be unable to repay investors. A bond is a loan by an investor to a company or a government.

international food operations and that was Reg's target.

Reg had the deal all figured out. Work with Milken and Drexel to borrow a lot of the money, put in very little of his own and win the bid for Beatrice International. He needed me to put together the PR plan and draft the news release. I left his home and almost stumbled down the steps. My head was spinning as I stepped out into the warm New York night and just breathed it all in. I decided to walk home. I lived on the Upper East Side, and it was about thirty blocks, but I was young and who was counting? I couldn't believe that this man whom I'd met just a month ago planned to take over one of the largest companies in the world by borrowing an enormous amount of money through Milken's junk bonds and win an international auction against all comers. It was big, bold, audacious. After all, no one had ever heard of TLC Group until that *Times* article. But what if he managed to pull it off?

That would make Reginald Lewis the most powerful and richest African American in the U.S., the CEO of a global corporation, and it would elevate me to a position of incalculable power and prestige.

4 – "I'M GOING TO REPORT YOU TO THE FACILITY MANAGER!" 1977 – 1983

A rise to the top of the American corporate world was the furthest thing from my mind when I first arrived in Gainesville, Florida, to start my studies. I wound up taking a $200 a month shack in the back of a huge empty house on the outskirts of the sprawling University of Florida campus. It was cheap and it gave me my privacy. I spent most of my time at the library studying and as a result, in 1979, I graduated from UF as the first-ever honors graduate of its Master's in Journalism and Communications program.

My next stop was Chicago where I became the one-person PR department for a group of nightclubs, La Margarita, where our main attraction aside from the flavorful mole dishes was an Elvis impersonator called Jimett. I'd replaced an old-timer named Jerry Conner who walked with a cane and whose version of PR was, "We're all whores, Butch; we go to the highest bidder." I managed to get my boss, the nightclub owner, on the front cover of the *Chicago Tribune*'s Sunday magazine, a feat of which I was justifiably proud.

I was celebrating at the Billy Goat Tavern one night with some reporters when Jimett, hair slicked back and decked out in a long-sleeved, flouncy white satin shirt and tight pants, sidled up to me. "Butch, I want a big story like that on me." He confided in me that the end of music lay just around the corner because "I don't believe that anyone can write any new songs." Why not, I asked. "Because there are only so many notes on the piano keyboard. All the good songs have been written, man." I told myself, "Time to go." I just couldn't continue to drum up publicity for Elvis impersonators and there was no way I'd ever get Jimett on the cover of the *Tribune*'s Sunday magazine.

I moved to San Francisco where I ground out marketing brochures for Bank of America. In one of the most scenic cities in the U.S., I'd cuddle up in bed on cold, foggy nights happily consuming Dashiell Hammett novels. But like so many others, America for me was New York City. It was the mecca of PR, the best place for me to find a job and break into the bigtime in my field, which I sorely wanted to do. One day in 1983, I took off for the Big Apple, without a job or connections of any kind.

At first, I slept on the couches of relatives in New Jersey. I also had a distant aunt who lived alone in the city. Eventually, a friend of a friend offered to illegally sublet to me a rent-controlled studio apartment on the East Side of Manhattan. The paint was peeling off the walls. I took time every evening to suddenly turn on the lights and tap dance on the floor to stamp out the cockroaches. I knew they'd survived for 100,000 years but I was bent on killing as many of them as I could. But it was in a nice neighborhood. I had saved a little money and used it to pay my expenses, living as frugally as I could.

The New York that I discovered was a city that was on its deathbed, having been on the brink of bankruptcy in 1975 and then getting hammered by a national recession in the early 1980s. The first day, I eagerly walked around, easing my way past the garbage that blocked the sidewalks and stank of rotting food. As I crossed a street, I was almost run over by a car, and the driver gave me a friendly New York welcome. "Fuck you!" he shouted as he gave me the finger.

A messenger on a bicycle who'd observed the incident offered me advice that I sorely needed and that I take to heart to this day. "You should say 'Fuck you, too.'" Now why didn't I think of that?

After walking a few blocks, my shirt was drenched in perspiration, and I decided that I needed a better brand of deodorant. I wandered over to Times Square, where I enjoyed mingling with the anonymous, aggressive multitude, pushing and shoving its way through the streets. Sex stores dotted the area and prostitutes smiled at me while slinking in the doorways. You could get your fortune told by gypsy ladies in dark rooms tucked onto side streets for $20. Many stores were closed permanently and shuttered tight by iron gates. People tiptoed around the bodies of the homeless trying to sleep and a crazy man chased after me, demanding money. When I refused to answer, he started yelling to everyone, "He can't speak English! He can't speak English!" in a bid to humiliate me.

New York's sewage system lay in disrepair, each week bringing news of yet another sixty-year-old water main bursting. Muggers patrolled the streets while recent residents of mental wards haunted subway stations. Stations stank of urine while the trains themselves struggled on, though slow and spattered with graffiti. Floors were stained by blotches of dirt that were like ink blots spilled at random or a bacterial alien outbreak ready to swallow up waiting passengers. Soda pop cans, half-eaten sandwiches, and paper bags littered the tracks that at night played host to squeaking, healthy-looking rats. And the New Yorkers who braved the subways, who day after day pushed their tired, ill-used bodies in and out of the trains? They looked used-up and unhappy, staring trance-like at posters of Florida or the Bahamas as if they'd rather be anywhere else but the city.

One day, I watched a kid snatch a tourist's shopping bag, then, as the tourist shouted for help and started to run after the thief, a second kid tripped him, and he fell to the pavement with a yelp. No one said a word or bothered to offer a hand. I briefly considered crossing the street and bopping the kid on the head with the wooden tennis racket I happened to be lugging at the time but thought better of it. There was something in me that wanted to help whenever I saw injustice or unfairness. Maybe that came from my parents, my Jesuit upbringing, or those movies I'd watched like *Shane* or *High Noon* where Alan Ladd or Gary Cooper always stood tall and fought for the defenseless. But it was in there somewhere and I felt it keenly, even if I failed to act on it that day.

Another afternoon, while loitering on a public bench near Rockefeller Center, I saw young men use rocks to bust locks and ride off with bicycles while nobody did a thing. Even the security guards paid no attention. Coming home late one night on the subway, I made the mistake of sitting in the first car alone. A gaggle of teenagers quickly surrounded me. One of them pointed at my watch. I tensed up and readied myself for a fight. Anxious seconds passed as we stared at each other. Then the train pulled into a station. Magically, the doors opened, and I got up to make my escape. There standing before me was a huge New York City cop, arms crossed, glaring at my companions. I was never so happy to see a policeman.

At night, the wailing sirens of police cars or ambulances serenaded me and, in the mornings, the clankety clank clank of the garbage trucks woke me. That was followed by the whirr of autos as people strove to maneuver them from one side of the street to another sometimes blocks away in order to avoid the city's fines for parking on a street on a cleaning day. A friend of mine parked his car all the way in Queens and traveled back to Manhattan by subway and then made the trip once a week to move it to the other side of the street to avoid the daily battle for a parking space.

Just playing tennis could be a stressful experience. In between looking for a job and wandering the streets and subways of Manhattan, I'd search out a game at the courts in Central Park which were cheap and hotly contested. I biked to the Park at 5:30 in the morning to beat everyone out to one of the precious venues. Some of the old geezers grumbled every time one of my balls floated over to their side. Another time, a lady who I was playing against complained about how many times I bounced the ball before serving.

"You're only supposed to bounce the ball three times before you serve."

"You've been counting how many times I bounce the ball? You've got to be kidding. I'm pretty sure that there's no such rule," I said and proceeded to bounce away.

"I'm going to report you to the facility manager!"

"Go ahead," I said as I served the ball extra hard in her direction. Another time, my opponent knocked me down with a wicked forehand aimed right at my head while I was guarding the net.

None of that mattered though. New York, while shabby and bedraggled, was still, well, New York. A certain gritty style, a pizazz and energy invigorated people, making them proud even in the face of decline. As the financial and communications center of the country, New York retained the power to make or break dreams. So, for me, as for millions of others, the city's flame still shone brightly as a beacon of hope. I knew that I had to do well in this strange metropolis or go back to Manila, which I did not want to do. Martial Law had become more brutal. Bodies turned up regularly in empty fields of cogon grass. One by one, my brother and my four sisters followed me to the U.S. to study there. One of them married a farmer's son from Iowa whom she met in school. Three of them settled in the U.S. when years later, Dad acquired U.S. citizenship because of his service in World War II. That was a game changer for all of us although I remember him teary-eyed when he gave up his Filipino citizenship. He'd done it for us so we could have a better life.

Besides, without even noticing it, I'd fallen in love ... with America. I liked watching Johnny Carson come on TV at 11:30 every weeknight. I relished catching a baseball game on TV. I took pleasure in the ability to hop on a Greyhound bus and travel three thousand miles to another coast. When you did well, people were genuinely happy for you, not secretly hoping you failed as was often the case in the Philippines. Coming from a country where there were huge disparities in income, I was encouraged by the fact that people in the U.S. earned a good living working with their hands; they didn't need to attend college to do OK; and they could go on vacations just like the rich, if perhaps not to the same places.

I liked their sense of humor, too. One night in Florida, I went out on a canoe with friends in a river known to have alligators. Suddenly, we heard a splash next to us and the fellow behind me whispered, "I'd say paddle would be a good idea right now, Butch."

I savored watching basketball or football games in bars, chatting up the bartender or even random strangers who were friendly and eager to tell me their life story. They told me more about themselves in ten minutes than I knew about my friends back home after going to school with them for sixteen years. I loved television plus the independence of being on my own. I reveled in the country's tolerance: "You can do anything you want as long as you don't bother other people," a California cousin of mine advised me.

I liked how people seemed so optimistic and they weren't afraid to speak their minds. Everyone's opinion was welcome, no matter where you came from. They were a generous people too, the kind who'd charge you less if they knew you were hard up or, in the days when it was safe to do so, pick somebody up on the highway and give them a lift. The shoeshine man in La Guardia Airport told me that I could use his shoeshine box to shine my shoes for free as often as I wanted even if he wasn't around.

Americans said what they meant; there was no subterfuge to them, although I discovered this wasn't true of everyone in New York. And they expected that same honesty from you. If you told them something, they believed you. Some might call them gullible but to me, they were candid and straightforward. The country even smelled different. I remembered opening up the presents my parents brought home from trips to America and sniffing an aroma of freshness and cleanliness that stamped them as made in the USA. I wanted to stay. To do that, I had to have a job.

I sent my résumé to all the PR firms and got the usual rejections. I scoured the Want Ads in the papers and wrote dozens of applications. I'd check the mailbox several times a day even when I knew there were no more deliveries, hoping and praying that I'd find the letter that would change my life. I only needed one company to say yes. But after months of looking, there was nothing. I despaired of ever finding employment and started thinking about my options.

I began to run low on money and started skipping meals. No more tennis games. To earn extra dollars, I answered an ad asking for volunteers to take part in a drug experiment. It paid a thousand dollars and all I had to do was spend three weekends at a hospital hooked up to a tube and get injected with a heart drug they were testing. The nurses took good care of me, and the Israeli doctor assured me that it was safe. The money was good, and I was blind to any danger. One thousand dollars could last me a long time. Besides, I got to watch TV and enjoy free meals while lying in bed.

I even dropped by a church and got down on my knees and prayed. Dear God, please help me get a job. I really need it. But You know what is best for me, Lord. In the end, let Your will be done. Amen.

Little did I know that my prayers would be answered in a big way.

5 — "WE'RE COMFORTABLE AT $950 MILLION, REG"

The day after my visit to Reg's place, I spoke to my boss at Burson Marsteller, Chris Atkins, about Reg's plan to take over Beatrice International, and he greenlighted it. "Go ahead. I'm not sure if Reg can pull this off but if he does, it's going to turn into a terrific account. And you, my friend, are going to have a hell of a career."

Reg's headquarters was at Lewis & Clarkson, a small law office with a deluxe address at 99 Wall Street. Cheap filing cabinets overflowing with stuffed folders lined the walls. The furniture was utilitarian and inexpensive. TLC Group was housed there as well. It was Reg's LBO vehicle. He and a couple of executives had their own offices but everyone else sat at these desks in a huge room. A constant hum of chatter hung over the office; sassy wisecracking alternated with serious questions about work.

Most of the planning and strategizing for the Beatrice bid involved just two people—Reg and Cleve Christophe. Cleve was our finance guy and he built the computer model that enabled TLC Group to bid for the food behemoth.

Cleve Christophe was a slim, extremely intelligent and polished African American, immaculately groomed in a shirt and tie. Cleve was an old friend of Reg's and in the early days, he became one of the first clients of his law firm. Reg had brought him on board just that June to beef up his team. He was Reg's equal in intellectual capacity and he was ambitious as anyone. Within days of his joining the firm, he was neck deep in the Beatrice deal.

There were many meetings. Reg would meet with people individually or in groups. He would scan the room, taking everyone's measure. Then he would begin.

"I've chosen each of you because you're supposed to be the best. We've had one big success—McCall Pattern. But Beatrice International is the bigtime, boys. So, for the next few weeks, nothing exists outside of this deal. Not your families. Not your beds. Nothing. And if anyone doesn't feel like putting out the effort, you'd better fucking leave now."

It was like a locker room speech before a game. We fixed our eyes on the coach.

"Cleve developed a computer model for how this transaction is going to work. Let's use it. How high can we bid? How can we structure this deal? I'll be counting on you, Cleve, to get this bid to the finish line. Carl, you and Cleve work with Arthur Kalish of Paul Weiss. He's the top tax attorney in New York. Taxes are going to be one of the keys to this deal. Get yourselves up to speed on the tax codes of all these countries. That's going to be critical when we sell them. Everett, get going and make some calculations. Kevin, Charles, go over all the material for these international companies. Make yourselves useful. Butch, where's that plan on how we announce this to the media? If there's one thing you've taught me, it's that the press can make or break a deal."

A chorus of "Yes, Reg," "Sure, Reg," was heard from all around the table except from Cleve. He was a proud man and refrained from joining in.

"I intend to bid, win and close Beatrice International. So, let's focus. No distractions. There's no prize for second place. Deidra, get me Dean Kehler at Drexel," he shouted at his secretary, Deidra Wilson, a young, well-dressed Black woman with a stylish hairdo, as he headed out of the room. The meeting was over.

It was all new to me but somehow, I felt at home. Each of us was a specialist in something: law, finance, accounting, PR. At least I had my own undisputed kingdom, small though it may be. It was a lean team, and we all had a role to play. From then on, I spent almost all my time with Reg and TLC Group. Chris turned a blind eye as I neglected my other clients. Of course, Burson billed Reg $350 an hour —we thought we were lawyers—which was nowhere near what I was getting paid and that helped. Burson turned a nice profit as long as I was on the account.

I had gotten to know Reg's team over the last month but now I began to spend a great deal more time with them. They were a mix of lawyers, finance people and accountants. He seemed to have purposefully put together a motley group of white guys and African Americans; but one thing was clear: everything revolved around him. He'd established the firm. His signature was on everyone's paycheck. His moods determined how each day would go.

There was Everett Grant who had interviewed me on the phone that first day. He always dressed in a white shirt and conservative tie and had an open, honest face. He looked like an accountant from Price Waterhouse, which is what he was. He was one of Reg's top financial guys. He spoke in a halting, shy manner, almost verging on a stutter.

Of course, where there was a Lewis, there had to be a Clarkson. Like that famed pair of American frontiersmen who'd tamed the West for the new nation, though, this Clarkson spoke with a Bronx accent and wore a beard. He had season tickets to Jets and Yankees games, although by 1987, the Mets had captured the World Series the year before and were rapidly becoming the city's team. The Yankees, like New York City, were in the middle of a prolonged slump. Charles Clarkson had joined Reg soon after he graduated from law school and had never worked anywhere else. He was one of the sweetest guys I'd ever met with a loud voice and a sarcastic sense of humor. He kept a jar of candies on his desk for anyone with a sweet tooth. Charles was also a hard worker and often spent evenings at the office sleeping on the floor. But Reg was clearly the boss.

Reg and Cleve would talk and argue the pros and cons of the bid late into the night.

"I told you, Reg," said Cleve. "Milken's the key. Without him, we don't have a credible offer. You've got to see him and get Drexel on board."

"Don't you think I fucking know that?"

"We've got to have him one way or another."

"I guess you're right. What time's the plane leave for LA, Deidra?" he yelled out the door.

"Ten p.m., Mr. Lewis. You're going to have to hurry if you're going to catch it."

"Where are we at right now?"

"We're pretty comfortable at a bid of $950 million dollars, Reg," Cleve responded.

"Kalish says we'll be saving on taxes in some of these countries when we start selling the businesses, Reg," Carl added.

This was exciting stuff. I'd never before been part of a transaction of this kind or size. Reg's plan was simple but by no means risk free. He intended to sell off all the Beatrice International companies to repay the debt except for a core centered in Western Europe that he viewed as the true gems of the group. Irish potato chips, French supermarkets, a Dutch beverage firm, ice cream companies that were market leaders in seven countries across the continent. They earned enough money to give him a steady cash flow that could service what would still be a crushing amount of debt, even after the sale of the other companies.

The important element of a leveraged buyout was exactly that. It was highly leveraged. The buyer only put in a small amount of actual money; most of it was borrowed and then repaid with the sale of the purchased company's assets. Reg and TLC had to structure their bid so that it was high enough to win but low enough that they could still repay most of the debt with the sale of the companies and service the rest of it with the earnings of the European core. The sum of $950 million was a lot of money for a kid from Manila, and I could tell it was a lot of money for each of the guys in that room. If they bid too low, they would lose the auction and have to eat all their immense expenses on outside law firms, accountants, investment banks. If they bid too high, it could wreck the whole deal and make it impossible for them to make money on it, bankrupting the entire enterprise. In a very real way, everyone's job was on the line.

6 – MISFITS, 1983-1985

In 1983 though, $950 million was a meaningless figure to me. I could barely scrape together enough money to pay for my rent.

One day, an acquaintance of mine from back home suggested that I apply at a small public relations company that he'd worked at. It was called Hoxter Inc. I followed his advice and was surprised when I came home one afternoon to find a letter asking me to come and work there. The salary was just $20,000 a year but I let out a big cheer when I got the news. There was a God after all.

Thus it was that I landed at Fifth Avenue and the corner of 57th street one morning to start work. The building boasted a gold-trimmed, ornately decorated grand façade but as soon as you walked in, you noticed that it had seen better days. There was a guard who doubled as a receptionist sitting lack-adaisically behind an old desk in the lobby. The elevators creaked and smelled musty but to me, it felt like the most exciting place in the world where big things happened every day. The sole proprietor and exalted leader of the company was Curtis Hoxter, a barrel-chested, bespectacled man who'd immigrat-ed from Germany, served in the U.S. Army in World War II and still spoke with a thick German accent. And oh yes, he was cross-eyed.

"Butch! Where are the newspapers? Why aren't they on my desk? Man-fred, what's going on here?" he yelled every morning. That was part of my job.

Manfred von Hartmuth was a tall personable Austrian of noble blood or so I imagined. He had a slight paunch, perhaps from too many good meals, and spoke slowly and softly. How he got to New York and why he worked with Hoxter was a mystery that I failed to decipher. "I'll tell you about it someday, Butch," he'd say.

He never uttered a peep when Hoxter shouted at him and yet he always managed to project a certain cultured air and dignity. It hung about him like cologne.

Hoxter cornered the market in handling financial PR for big European companies. I was one of his account executives. We wrote press releases and attempted to get positive stories about our clients. We organized meetings with investment analysts and reporters. The goal was to enhance the German or Austrian company's image in the American business community, particularly Wall Street since many of these corporations invested or borrowed money in the U.S. Many were public companies in their home countries, and favorable press helped attract investors and seal deals.

Hoxter loved to hold functions at the Metropolitan Club. It was this grand building that stood proudly on Fifth Avenue with the flags of France, Britain, Germany and other nations hanging from its walls. A red canopy entrance on 59th street led you into a huge hall with a wood-paneled ceiling and a large candelabra staring at you, asking "Do you belong here?" The Club was a refuge for old money and elegance in a city that teemed with people from every nation.

"You know they never used to let Jews in here?" he told me once. So it was with a mixture of pride and bravado that he, Curtis Hoxter, a German-American Jew would stride in and make himself at home there with no one able to object to his presence.

"Butch, where's the release on the Austrian Stock Exchange?"

"I'm almost done with it, Mr. Hoxter."

"I need it right away! MAANFRED, have we hired a bunch of dumbbells! Where's Manfred? He's never in his office!"

Hoxter's crossed eyes bore into me. Once, he picked up a brochure and threw it at me. Another time, he crumpled pieces of paper into balls that he'd lob at me. I always ducked just in time. I doubted anyone ever read those reports on the Austrian Stock Exchange. However, under pressure, I learned to write quickly and succinctly. I had come a long way to be with Hoxter and I was determined to hang on and make it work.

There were weeks when we worked without any drinking water since Hoxter refused to pay for the gallon jugs of spring water we ordered.

"When are you going to pay the water bill, Mr. Hoxter? I've got a kidney condition," complained Helen Wasserstein, one of the secretaries. Playing Marie Antoinette, he replied, "Drinking water? We have no obligation to provide drinking water. What's wrong with tap water? Take it up with Manfred. Where is our Austrian Speedy Gonzales?"

Helen walked over to me. She worked to bring in extra cash because her husband Marty was retired. "I need the major medical in case Marty has an operation." She only had two topics of conversation. One was the coming wedding of her daughter to a rich Jewish doctor from Miami. The wedding of the century. Catered, with a band yet. Her other topic was how bad it was at Hoxter Inc.

"Learn what you can, then get out. He's just a basic bastard. He's Jewish, but I don't consider him Jewish. I don't consider him anything. Do you know that when his first wife died, may she rest in peace, he went through the ceremonies and only stayed home for a day before he was back in the office carrying on. And on the day he was out, he called the office every five minutes. I'll tell you something. Hoxter's biggest regret is that he wasn't born blond and blue eyed. He really doesn't consider himself a Jew. That's why when he remarried, he got himself a Shiksa, a blond mousy type. Remember what I said Butch, there's a lot you can learn here but there's no reason to stay."

On the back of the door to our filing room was a poem, typed up on a yellowed and crinkled sheet of paper, like a message from a long-gone prisoner.

We the willing, led by the unknowing,
Are doing the impossible, for the ungrateful.
We have done so much, for so long,
with so little. We are now qualified,
To do anything, with nothing.[4]

Next to it was penned the protest, "Says who?" and next to that a response, "Says the Willing!"

Everybody was a character. There was Renata, a Holocaust survivor with a number in purple tattooed on her wrist from her years at a concentration camp in World War II and violet hair from a bad dye job.

"Only my mother and I survived the camps. The Nazis took all our possessions, the house, the car, the furniture. My mother still finds things that belonged to us. At a party once, she found an antique chair of ours. Her friends were very embarrassed and apologized and said they'd bought it at an auction and had no idea where it came from. They were apologetic and offered to return the chair, but my mother refused. We lived through terrible times, but I make them pay for it to this day," she winked at me. "Every time I sneeze, I say to myself, oops that's 50 cents the Germans owe me. They still pay me a pension, you see. So I've survived worse things than this pig. And I'm still here."

[4] Quote from Konstantin Jirecek, Czech politician of the late 19th and early 20th century.

There was Debbie, the black receptionist who had no problem answering Hoxter back, "It's not my fault, Mr. Hoxter!" Ann, the Georgia peach who'd transformed herself into a tough and fashionably dressed New Yorker, "Butch, never take the subway. It's too depressing." Tommy Tiptop Clohesy from Schenectady, an Irish American graduate of the Institute of Strategic Studies in Washington who spoke German. Eddie, the Puerto Rican messenger who moonlighted as a stripper, "Did I tell you about the time this one woman grabbed my balls so hard I screamed?" Beverly Whitney or Witless as we sometimes called her, the daughter of a New York magnate who was our supposed office manager, "Has everyone filled out their time sheets this week?"

Above us all hung the specter of Curtis Hoxter. "MAANFRED, where is the Thyssen file? No one has any idea what's going on. Am I surrounded by nitwits!" This was my world and my introduction to New York every morning.

Two years flew by. Then one day, I consoled yet another Hoxterite, a Black Princeton graduate, as tears streamed down his face after yet another bout of screaming from the boss. "What are you still doing here, Butch?" he asked. "You're too good for this place." I didn't say anything, but decided he was right. I had learned a great deal, but I was ready to move on and to finally free myself from Hoxter's grasp.

In the end, like almost everyone else, I left Hoxter for a much bigger PR firm, Ruder Finn & Rotman, that had floors packed with account executives. My salary jumped to $40,000 just like that. When I told Hoxter and Manfred the news, they didn't look surprised. Nobody stayed very long.

The Flying Viking

My new bosses were Harriet Mouchly-Weiss, a woman who seemed bigger than life and was the epitome of a Jewish mother. She had a loud voice, a big smile and the kind of personality that enveloped everyone in the room in its embrace and could charm you into walking out onto a high-rise scaffolding without a safety net. Then there was Norman Weissman, who wore glasses and kept himself trim by walking every day from the upper eighties on the West Side all the way down to our offices on Third and 55th. I was a young immigrant, and they gave me a chance.

At an agency, you handle several accounts, sort of like juggling balls. There was a wide range of clients. One of my accounts was someone called "The Flying Viking." He was this Swedish guy who flew high up in the air powered by a rocket strapped to his back, performing at circuses and outdoor concerts.

Harriet was on my case to get him press coverage because we had a partnership with a Swedish PR firm whose client he was. It didn't have to be *The Wall Street Journal*. Anything would do. The Swedes assigned a fellow by the name of Lars Wahlstrom to us so he could learn how things were done in New York and keep an eye on their clients. We in turn passed on our clients that needed PR in Europe to the Swedish firm. We established these relationships in different parts of the world so that we became a global agency and could service our customers no matter where they went. Lars was my main contact with the Viking, who could barely speak English.

"C'mon, Butchie," Harriet kept telling me. "You're good at this. Get somebody to do a story on the Viking."

I wrote pitch letters that tickled the media's interest. I followed them up with phone calls. One day, I got lucky. I got the rocket man a stint on *The Regis Philbin Show*, which at the time was the city's number one morning TV program. My idea was that he would soar high above Central Park, thrilling TV viewers and scaring the heck out of anyone who happened to be at the park that morning.

"I like it. I like it," the show's producer chanted. The local ABC station heavily promoted the stunt. "Join us for the Flying Viking as he flies above Central Park" ran the jingle that played constantly on TV. The only problem was that the night before, he was scheduled to wing his way above the football stadium in New Jersey before a huge crowd celebrating Independence Day. That part went well.

The next morning, I woke up early to get everybody to Central Park. I was irritated to find Lars fast asleep when I stopped by to pick him up. I waited for him to come to the door and that's when I got the bad news. As he rubbed his eyes, he mumbled something about the Flying Viking not being able to go to the Park that day. I couldn't believe my ears and started to get upset.

"What do you mean, Lars? Everything is all arranged. I confirmed it with you last night! The ABC crew is already at Central Park. There's a crowd gathered there to watch. Is this the way you do things in Sweden?"

"I'm sorry, Butch. Most of his fuel was used up during last night's show. He doesn't have enough left to make the flyover at the Park."

"How about if he just goes up and down? Just once. Can we get fuel from a gas station? C'mon, Lars; I'm dead if this doesn't happen."

"It's aviation fuel. It's not the same gasoline that cars use."

"How could he use up all the fuel when he knew we were doing this show? It's the top program in New York and reaches millions."

"I can't explain it," Lars threw up his hands helplessly.

I wanted to kick the garbage can or strangle Lars. I couldn't decide which would give me more satisfaction. To make a long story short, the Flying Viking would not fly over Central Park or anywhere else that day.

The show's producer was livid. "Goddamn you! We've been promoting this for days. I promise you that you will never, ever book anything on this program again!"

Such were the perils of my chosen profession. This had been a huge opportunity to get my client on a big-time show. To be shut out of *Regis Philbin* could hurt my career. To my relief, both Harriet and Norman were sympathetic. Public relations in New York can be a tough business with a great deal of shouting and cursing, but they weren't like that. In that sense, I was lucky, and I strove harder to meet or exceed their expectations.

"Don't worry, Butch," Harriet said. "It wasn't your fault."

The Prime Minister of Jamaica

Our biggest client, however, was a different animal. It was the government of Jamaica. We did everything for them that the CIA might. We sent a team of political operators to Kingston, the capital, and they set up shop down the hallway from the Prime Minister's office. That way, they were always accessible to him and could keep tabs on what was happening. One key adviser sat in on almost all of the important meetings.

The Prime Minister was Edward Seaga, who was close to President Reagan and the U.S. at a time when they saw Communist Cuba as a major threat in the Caribbean. Seaga and his staff turned to us for advice on just about everything. We established the Jamaican Information Service, or JIS, which ran the government news agency and TV station. There were JIS attachés in every embassy to help spread the good word. "Come back to Jamaica" ran the ads of our multimillion-dollar campaign. They worked. Tourist arrivals jumped. We supervised everything from New York. We functioned as if we were part of the government, which some Jamaicans resented, as I was told bluntly at cocktail parties.

"Why are you doing this, man? You're not Jamaican."

I was everywhere. I wrote some of the Prime Minister's speeches and the press releases hyping Blue Mountain coffee and the Jamaican economy. I prepared a monthly analysis for him of American press coverage of Jamaica and advised him on how to handle issues such as drugs or street protests. I traveled to Kingston, the capital, to attend Cabinet meetings and accompanied the Prime Minister on his periodic trips to Washington to ask for money from the International Monetary Fund. He always had to have a pint of Butter Pecan ice cream before he went to bed. No other flavor would do.

The Prime Minister was fundamentally a shy person, which was odd for a politician. He wasn't into small talk. Light-skinned, elegant, and refined, he spoke with a touch of an English accent. He always wore a suit, his hair carefully combed back. He never let his guard down and it was hard for me to get to know him.

"Now, Butch, this is what I'd like the release to say," he'd tell me as we sat in the study of his hotel room in New York. I figured that he came from one of these old Jamaican families who had grown wealthy during colonial times. Sometimes, the PM would host top-secret meetings with shady financiers like Marc Rich, who ended up fleeing the U.S. for Switzerland after tax evasion charges. He hid out there for years—"We really miss the pizza" is what one of his associates told reporters—till President Clinton pardoned him on his last day in office. Jamaica possessed valuable minerals like bauxite, copper and iron that attracted investors far more than the pretty beaches.

Unfortunately, no matter how many glowing press releases we sent out, our man just wasn't very popular. He was conservative in an economic sense. He borrowed billions of dollars from the IMF and that meant going along with their hardline austerity policies, like cutting back on social spending. There were riots in the streets of Kingston over rising gas prices. No gain without pain, we'd say, and in time, I came to believe it. I had to if I was going to do my job. For PR to work, you have to believe in the individual or the institution that you're promoting. It's not like you're selling soap. I knew that the Prime Minister's policies were hurting ordinary Jamaicans, but I believed what he said—that he was guiding the economy through a difficult time and that all the sacrifices would eventually pay off in a better life for everyone. After all, I was writing his speeches.

Public relations can do many things, but it can't turn water into wine. An election was called and Seaga was voted out. It wasn't good for the U.S. because Jamaica took a sharp turn to the left and began cozying up to Cuba. It was terrible for the agency. The first thing the new Prime Minister did was fire us, which is what happens in the PR game. When a new CEO takes over a company or in the case of a government account, a new head of state assumes power, one of the first things they do is let go of the PR team. They always want their own people around them, not somebody else's, even if we'd have happily switched sides if the money was right.

We let go of many of our staff in both Kingston and New York who worked on the Jamaica account. But I got to stay. It was those big stories that I placed in *The Wall Street Journal* on behalf of our clients. I was at home with reporters, and I was a good salesman. I had acted in plays, TV shows and movies when growing up in Manila and that helped. I knew how to pitch a story. And as Barbara Burns, one of my former bosses, once remarked about me, "He writes like an angel."

We continued to stick with our man, although at a much-reduced budget; the former PM was now head of the opposition. I had the unenviable task of trying to get reporters in the U.S. to write about his gigantic memoirs. The Prime Minister had been working on them for years and the book was heavy enough to give you a hernia if you carried it. I bravely soldiered on, promoting the magnum opus with the American press. But it was no use. They had moved on and there is nothing deader than a has-been. I'd accompanied Edward Seaga to the gates of the White House and the elegant hotels of New York. *Forbes* magazine did stories on him, courtesy of me. But now no one was interested in a former Jamaican Prime Minister. "Who cares?" the media told me.

I contemplated leaving Harriet and Norman. They'd already shepherded some 15 of us along with our accounts from Ruder Finn to GCI Group, the PR arm of Grey Advertising. It was an exodus that made Page One of *The Wall Street Journal*. Finally, I myself left the new agency to join Burson Marsteller for a small increase in salary. GCI's CEO, Fran Friedman, asked me to reconsider.

"We don't work in public relations to get rich, Butch," she told me. But by then, I'd already seen her multi-acre, Connecticut home with a pond during an office party. So I shrugged her off.

I nursed this constant urge, this ambition, to take another step up the ladder of success. I was young and unafraid. What I didn't realize was that I was on the cusp of achieving everything and more than I'd ever thought possible when I first set foot in the tawdry avenues of Times Square.

7 – MIKE MILKEN

"Let's go over the mechanics once more," Reg said, and slammed his fist on the desk. "We gotta be sure. We're up against some pretty big boys—Citicorp, that French food conglomerate, Bon Grain—and we'll need a bigger bat to swing with. That's where Mike Milken and Drexel come in."

"OK, Reg. Let me walk you through the deal," said Cleve.

"You'll walk me through the deal?" Reg bristled. "Who the fuck do you think you are anyway, Cleve? TLC Group is my company and Beatrice is my transaction. Do I make myself clear?"

Reg's moods could swing in an instant. He was under tremendous pressure. Cleve just stared at him, and I could tell he wasn't like the rest of us. He wouldn't put up with the tantrums. Reg shouted, "I'm going to LA!" And with that, he put on his coat, grabbed his briefcase, and started to rush out the door.

Like all the other big investment banks, Drexel was headquartered in New York. But as a concession to its main rainmaker, as they call someone who makes a lot of money for the firm, Drexel established a Los Angeles outpost, right in the middle of Beverly Hills. Mike Milken was that important to them and no accommodation was too much to please him.

In his heart, I was told, Mike was a California guy, and it didn't matter to him that he and his team on the West Coast had to be in the office at 4:30 or 5 in the morning so they could keep up with the New York crew. They willingly made the sacrifice, maybe giving up their weeknights partying and anything else that was too late at night. There was just too much money to be made and living out West suited them, because although they had to come in early, the compensation was that they could perhaps leave early. Because after the markets closed and people in New York were busy waging war with the traffic or the subway system, they had time to catch their kids' baseball games or shop or engage in hobbies like learning French or taking yoga classes.

Milken arranged for breakfast, lunch, and dinner to be served to everyone at the office, for free. There was always food around. So, really, there was never any reason to leave the premises. Everyone worked in this one huge trading room, at the center of which was the man who'd built the firm and ran their lives and paid their big bonuses—Mike at his X-shaped desk, on the phone, leaning over to talk to someone, in perpetual motion.

Reg was ushered into a large office set off to the side. He could look out on the floor with the vast number of traders pursuing deals. This was the headquarters of Takeover, Inc. Here, Drexel provided access to capital through their junk bonds to companies all across America that were below investment grade. The total junk bond market was worth $150 billion at one point. Drexel shook up the corporate world and fueled the overthrow of the elite. All an entrepreneur needed was a letter from one man saying that he was highly confident that the transaction could be financed. The letter wasn't legally binding but Milken's imprimatur was so respected, that was all that was required to clinch a deal. It all began here, with that one man. And as Reg waited, that man strolled in.

He had dark hair (we only found out later that he wore a wig), was of medium height and had eyes that seemed to see right through you. He projected a kind of hyperactive dynamism, intelligence, and vigor. Beside him was his right-hand man in whose hands was a copy of the "90 to One" article from the *Times*.

"Reg, you know Peter Ackermann, right?"

Reg nodded at him.

"That was a great job on McCall, Reg," Milken said as he sat down at his desk. Reg and Peter remained standing. He got right down to business. "Maybe we can give you more firepower. How much money did you make? $75 million?" (He was guessing.)

"I did pretty well," Reg said, waving his hand in the air as if it was no big deal, although his face glowed with pride. To Milken though, whatever the amount, it was small potatoes. That year alone, in 1987, he made over $550 million.

"I think it's time to get serious, Reg. Let's take this show to Broadway. Where have all the great fortunes been made? Real estate, oil, finance. You have to ask yourself, what is it you really want? What are you chasing? You could be another Rockefeller, Rothschild, JP Morgan. Just think of it." Reg stared at Milken intently. Ackermann stood watching quietly.

"I know you, Reg. We're two of a kind. We're winners. For people like us, money is just a way of keeping score. Companies belong to those who are willing to take risks. Drexel is leveling the playing field so anyone with the guts and the ambition can go after General Motors, IBM, you name it. We're going to tee them all up and we're going to make them cringe."

It was quite a speech. Milken was much more than the greedy SOB that some in the media portrayed him. He was a revolutionary, out to evict the staid old corporate patricians and let in the tumultuous horde. He wanted to democratize wealth. Even an outsider like Reg could scale the barricades.

Reg told them about Beatrice International. At first, they seemed dubious, but Reg persisted. He had put everything he had mentally and emotionally into the deal. His future and that of the rest of the team at TLC Group depended on the outcome of this one meeting.

"I've got a plan," Reg said. He was fired up. "Bid for the whole thing at 950. Then sell Canada for $200 million, Australia for $100 million, Latin America for $100 million. That's just for starters. We've still got Asia to sell. We'll pare it down to the European core; that's where the money is anyway."

They were unconvinced. Mike sat behind his desk, king of all he surveyed. He barked out a series of questions. Why should we back you? How are we going to make money? Tell me more about the Beatrice operations. If Reg was intense, Milken was even more intense and focused. But Reg had studied everything about the deal. He answered every question without hesitation. Milken later said that he was surprised that Reg knew more about Beatrice than he did.

"You're not giving us a lot of time to raise the financing," Peter said, beginning to take over the conversation.

"That's why I came to the best," Reg said. "Your guys told me you could raise that kind of money in a phone booth."

"You're asking us to raise almost a billion dollars," Peter said. "We've never done business with you before. Why the hell would we go out on a limb for you?"

"I just told you," Reg said. "You'll never have to raise a billion. We've got buyers for Canada, Australia, and Latin America. It's all pre-sold."

"You got any contracts?" Peter put his hands on his hips.

"No, of course I don't have any contracts yet, but I've got the buyers lined up." Reg waved his arm at him as if it was no big deal and the businesses were as good as sold.

"The fact is that you're asking us to take a very substantial risk," Peter pressed.

"And getting well paid for it! You're going to get $35 million in fees when this is over."

"Don't look into our pockets, Reg," Peter said.

"Yeah? Don't look into mine."

They briefly glared at each other. Milken was quiet.

"Reg, let's be clear," Peter said. "Without us, you wouldn't even be in the running." Peter looked like he was foaming at the mouth, with saliva spraying the air.

Milken sat back, watching them go at it, letting it all play out.

"You'd be the first Black man to be a member of our little club."

"Hell, why are you bringing up my ethnicity, Peter? I don't bring up your Jewishness!"

That left everyone quiet. Then Peter started to pace back and forth.

"We think we deserve stock in the company," he said.

"Stock? Your guys never mentioned this before," Reg seethed.

"We want 51 percent," Peter persisted.

"51 percent! What the hell are you trying to do, Peter? Take over my company before I've even got it? I'm not some goddamn Drexel puppet. You can fucking forget it!"

"It isn't your company yet, Reg. It may never be your company at all unless we help you out."

"I'm not giving away control. This is a TLC deal all the way." Reg needed them; he didn't have a chance without them, but he wasn't going to let anyone run his firm.

"Listen to me, you motherfucker; I will not participate in this deal unless I control it."

He took a step toward Peter. Reg was a burly guy, shorter than Peter but he looked like the ex-quarterback he had been in college. Peter was slim and didn't look athletic at all. But he didn't move an inch.

"Just who the fuck do you think you're kidding, Lewis? Face it. Without us, you don't have a deal."

"Go ahead," Reg said in a menacing whisper. "Pull out."

Peter took a step back, a surprised look on his face. "You're bluffing. This is the deal of a lifetime. It's going to put you in the big leagues. You're not going to walk away from all that."

"Pull out and see if I give a goddamn."

They stood face to face. The only thing missing were the gun holsters around their waists.

"Is this your idea, Mike?" Reg said without taking his eyes off Peter.

Mike was still for what seemed like a long time. Finally, he intervened.

"Ease up, Peter. What we're doing is, we're backing Reg."

With a reluctant shrug, Peter turned away. The tension lifted just a little.

"What do you think your chances are, Reg?" Mike said.

"Excellent, if we can get one those 'highly confident' letters from you."

"I'll tell you what," Mike said. "How about if we take 36 percent of the company? That seems fair. We're taking a serious risk and our investors like to participate in the upside."

"How much money are you comfortable raising, Mike?"

"We'll raise whatever you need."

"Talk to me, Mike," Reg said. "How much are you comfortable raising?"

Mike thought for a moment, his brow creased in thought. "About $500 million."

"Fine. I promise you that you'll never have to raise more than 500. We'll take care of the rest."

"If you don't pre-sell some of Beatrice's assets by the closing deadline, we're looking at a very different deal," Peter interjected.

Reg turned to Mike. "Where the hell did you get this guy, Michael? He's a wild man. I'm surprised you get any deals done at all. Listen, I'm a reasonable man. How about if we give you guys a 26 percent stake in the company at say, 25 cents a share?"

Peter rolled his eyes and grunted.

"Look, we found the deal," Reg said. "We're doing all the work. What do you say, Mike?"

Mike hesitated. Then he stood up, rubbed his hands together and began to turn toward the door.

"OK, Reg. We'll get the paperwork to you. Now I guess we'd better get out of your hair and let you bag this thing. Let's go, Peter."

8 – A CANDY CANE VISION OF AMERICA

Sometime after he got back to New York, Reg invited me over to his place. It was only then that I finally met Loida Nicolas Lewis. I had only spoken to her on the phone twice—first when she called me to help her husband with his PR problem and then after I scored the 90-to-one *New York Times* story on Reg. But I had never actually met her. I think Reg wanted to make sure we didn't get to know each other too well. No Filipino alliances here. He wanted me to be loyal to him and him alone.

Loida had met Reg on a blind date when she was visiting the U.S. after graduating from law school. Her sister was dating someone who was Reg's friend and she'd asked her to come along. It was to be one of the most successful blind dates in history.

Loida was a slim, dark-haired woman, tall for a Filipina. She was born in the province of Sorsogon in the Philippines. Her father nursed dreams of her someday running for senator so he named his movie theater after her so she could get some name recognition. While working at the U.S. Immigration Service, she had sued them for discrimination. She could be a strong-willed woman in her own right, but all that was hidden and beneath the surface when Reg was around. He was the star of the show. Everyone else was just part of the supporting cast. Loida played the role of the docile corporate wife. She seemed to be content to be his cheerleader and sounding board.

"It was a rough meeting with Drexel, but I think I showed them who was boss. Fuck those guys," he blurted out. "We'll get this deal done one way or the other."

Reg sank into a chair.

"They're bastards, Loida. That's for sure. But I liked Mike."

"You look tired."

"I'm fine. But I need to get this deal done. I can feel it in my bones that this is the right one. I can't think of anything else. This deal is eating me up. After all the failures, Beatrice can get me into the big time; it'll give us a chance to build one of the great American fortunes, Loida."

"You'll get it, darling. I'm going to pray hard for it. God is good."

Loida was pretty religious.

"I'm going to need all the help I can get. We're going to have to put in millions in the deal ourselves."

I realized that Reg was putting in his own money in the transaction. Unlike the McCall deal, he wasn't asking any of his friends for help.

"All these years of lawyering for small-time fees, doing fucking MESBIC[5] deals that they hand out as tokens to minority law firms, then the fucked-up California transaction. I knew I wasn't ready then; so, I told myself to get ready. Then McCall happened. I wasn't some kind of overnight success. This was more than twenty years in the making. And if Beatrice doesn't work, I'm not sure I'll be able to recover."

Loida took him in her arms. "I'll always be there for you, Reg. But don't worry. You're going to get it."

Reg pulled away and gave her a hard look. "What do you know about LBOs?"

"I don't know anything about them," Loida answered coolly. "But I know you. And I know you're going to take Beatrice."

"You've always been a winner, Reg," I added helpfully.

He glared at us.

"Neither of you understand. When you're Black in this country, they lead you to the water, but they won't let you drink. What I have, I've had to fight for every inch of the way. As a Black man, I don't just want a seat at the table. I want to sit at the head of the table. You Filipinos have this candy cane vision of America that doesn't exist."

The dam burst. "I think all Filipinos are racists basically, although I never sensed that with you, Butch," he said. He accused me of viewing the U.S. through the lens of the Hollywood movies I'd grown up on. That I didn't really understand how racist things were in the U.S.

"You don't know. But every Black guy worth his salt grows up with a sense of anger. Every day, I'm out there on the field, throwing passes or rushing for a touchdown. And every time I score, I kick the shit out of the lie that ignorant people believe. That Blacks aren't good enough. You can be as rich as anyone but anytime a cop pulls you over, you know that you've got to be extra careful."

I wanted to say something in defense of my compatriots but in my heart,

---

[5] MESBIC stands for Minority Enterprise Small Business Investment Company. MESBICs were started by U.S. President Nixon in 1969 to invest in minority-owned firms as a way to assist minorities gain economically. They generally had a poor track record.

I knew there was a kernel of truth in Reg's words. He and Loida had gotten married in a historic outdoor park in Manila, and I could imagine the snide comments from the Manila glitterati that Reg probably picked up on. Maybe it was all the years of being a colony of both Spain and the U.S. but people tended to look down on those who were dark-skinned. When I was a boy, it seemed that only Americans got to sit in the balcony section of movie houses although that's where I sat. Perhaps because they were more expensive. Most of the Filipinos were in the orchestra seats.

I had my own problems. Walking the streets in the States sometimes or standing in line at supermarket checkout counters, I'd hear the casual insults, "Chink" or "I'm not prejudiced. You can go ahead of me." I wanted to tell them, I'm not Chinese; I'm Filipino and who do you think you are anyway. But I usually just let it go. Not worth getting into trouble, I told myself. In contrast, the racism at the top was never overt; it was much more subtle. The patronizing manner the secretaries treated you when you showed up at particular investment banks. The way they looked at you or pretended you weren't there.

There were certain companies that a Burson executive told me were "white shoe firms,"—mostly law firms or banks—which I took to mean that they would never hire someone like me nor would Burson assign me to handle their PR. But it was a different kind of battle for Reg. I began to understand that for him, race was a daily, all-consuming preoccupation, a war that he had to fight every time he walked out the door of his home or showed up at a meeting or ate at a restaurant. Was the slow service a slight to be avenged? Was there some reason we were seated next to the toilet? It fueled an inner rage in him that belied any attempt to relax or take things easy. He never let anything that smacked of racism pass unchallenged. When a white man would backslap him in a gesture that he regarded as patronizing, he stuck out his hand and hit him back as hard as he could to the point that left the other guy gasping for breath.

Much later, I got a firsthand glimpse of what he meant. There was one time on Fifth Avenue when the Bentley wasn't around that Reg almost got into a fight with a white man over a cab.

"We hailed him first," he told the man.

"I had my hand out well before you."

Meanwhile, the Indian taxi driver motioned that he wanted the white guy as his passenger. After a standoff, Reg let the guy have the cab.

"Never mind, we'll walk," he told me. Then he added with disgust, "I can see you'll be a lot of help if I ever get into a fight."

Loida and I were quiet, and he looked like he wanted to say more. I braced myself. But then he took off his tie.

"I've had enough for one day. Good night."

And with that, he got up, threw himself on the nearby couch, rolled over and fell asleep. Loida fetched a blanket which she gently laid over him. She nodded at me to let me know I could go home now.

9 – 1985, AT LONG LAST LOVE

During those early days in New York, I harbored dreams about being a writer. The city lent itself to that ambition. Bookstores flourished every few blocks, warm cozy places where one could linger. I worked on a novel about Hoxter and populated it with the characters I'd met there. I planned to call it *Misfits*, till someone reminded me that Arthur Miller had already penned a movie script by that name. I'd write these scenes about life at a New York public relations firm that I thought were hilarious. I rummaged through the office files on weekends and found old cards from the wake of Hoxter's wife, who'd died young, and incorporated that into my plot.

I yearned to write more than press releases. I think that I'd always had an urge to write a book because that was one of the few ways to achieve a kind of immortality. A book survived its author, even if today that book might only be published on the internet. Besides, writing was an outlet for my loneliness. New York City can be a special place, but it can also be a place where you have to hide your tears when you walk down the street because there may not be a sympathetic ear to whom you can tell your troubles or ask for advice. Writing gave me a sense of purpose and something to do during my spare time. I had this single-minded focus on the job and my writing, and I even worked on Saturdays. People headed to the beach or to the ball game would spot me lugging my briefcase and shout, "C'mon man, don't do that today."

I cherished the New York Public Library's huge high-ceilinged study rooms, each desk accented by Carrere and Hastings reading lamps with their brass shades hanging over the long wooden desks. My fellow scholars and writers toiled intently while above us towered murals depicting biblical scenes. Anyone speaking above a whisper was quickly shushed into silence. I wrote page after page about my life in New York. When I was tired, I grabbed a book on the Byzantine Empire from the shelves and lost myself in the bygone world of long-forgotten emperors assassinating each other. The library was a refuge and a safe haven for solitary souls like me. And it was a great place to hang out for free.

One Fourth of July, I happened to be standing on Fifth Avenue in front of the library, holding on tightly to a book of Neil Simon's plays that I'd checked out. In those days, I would carry a book with me all the time. Come to think of it, I still pack one whenever I travel. All of a sudden, my friend Gil Portes strolled by and caught sight of me. I had not seen him for years and didn't even know he was in New York. He was a famous movie director back home. I had worked with him during my internship at a TV studio in Manila and I eventually played roles in three of his films.

"Imagine running into you on the street in the middle of New York City on the Fourth of July!" He looked pleased to see me. Meeting him out of the blue in a city of over 12 million added to my sense that fate had a hand in that day's events.

"Want to come along to this party? It's at Sutton Place." He winked at me. "A truly maaavelous apartment that overlooks the East River. We can watch the fireworks from there."

"Whose party is it?"

"Some rich guy connected with President Marcos. He's not around but his nieces are and they're having a fireworks party. I know someone who's going to be there."

I started to get suspicious. "Do you know the hosts? Are you even invited?"

"No. But what does it matter? Like I said, I know one of the people who's going."

"What makes you think they're going to let us in?"

"Have a little faith in me, Butch. We'll get in. C'mon. It'll be fun."

I thought things over. I wasn't normally the kind of guy who gatecrashed a party, but I decided, what the heck? It was the Fourth of July and I had nothing else to do.

The buildings on Sutton Place were pretty fancy. A long, green awning welcomed us just before we entered. I admired the Roman busts adorning the lobby. The floor was made of dark wood. I began to wonder if this was a good idea. First, we had to get past the doorman.

"We're here to see Ms. Cruz," Gil said a little snootily and without a trace of doubt in his voice.

"You're here for the party?" the doorman asked and rang someone on the intercom. Surprisingly, he told us, "Go right ahead."

We jumped on the elevator and went right up to the penthouse. Gil pressed the doorbell, once, twice. He tried the heavy wooden door, but it was locked. I gave him a look and thought, "I should have stuck with Neil Simon." Then we heard someone fumbling with the knob and the door swung open and there before me was someone who appeared as if she was a princess of this castle on Sutton Place. She said her name was Pamela, but to me she seemed like a Filipina version of Leslie Caron, the French movie star. She looked very young and was friendly without any airs or trace of affectation. Her hair hung down to her shoulders and her dress was simple but stylish in an Annie Hall sort of way. After Gil told her, "We were invited by Marshall Factora," she let us in without question. I was used to closing up my apartment with triple locks so I was surprised at the ease with which we were able to waltz in and figured to myself she must be new to New York.

The condo boasted several bedrooms and a balcony that looked out at the East River. Off to one corner stood a Steinway piano. As we made our way inside, we discovered a handsome library and a wide selection of record albums. I hadn't been to any posh New York apartments like this one and I was impressed. Nice place to live, I told myself.

As soon as we entered, Gil went up to different people to chat them up or give them a hug.

"I'm Gil. That's suuuch a pretty dress. Where'd you get it?"

Gil made himself at home, as he usually did. He acted as though he knew everyone there and made a point of trying out every single piece of furniture, sitting on each chair or sofa, touching every table, turning on lamps. After a couple of bottles of beer, I relaxed and hung out with everyone. It was a mix of Filipinos from back home and Americans. The Filipinos were, as the phrase goes, all "from good families," and there was always some kind of connection, through school or the family.

Gil told jokes that he at least believed were funny as he bounced around the spacious apartment. He acted as though he were the host and everyone else was his guest. Marshall (which I'm pretty sure was an Americanized version of the Filipino name Marcial), an actor friend of Gil's, was gracious and introduced us to people. Marshall possessed an impressive résumé of roles as an extra in Hollywood movies and TV series. When the time came, we crowded onto the balcony, wine glasses and beer bottles in hand, to watch the multi-colored explosions of fireworks dance wildly over the water. I enjoyed being in such an exquisite apartment and it seemed like heaven to me to watch the Fourth of July fireworks from its balcony. Then Marshall played the piano and we all gathered around to sing Broadway songs. I even broke away in the middle of the night to wake up that aunt of mine who lived in the city some twenty blocks away so I could grab some sheet music and take it back to the party. I wanted to keep the party going so I could have more time with Pam. Marshall could play just about anything, as long as he had a sheet of music in front of him.

An older woman scratched my back and asked me for a date. But most of my attention was on Pam. She was like a breath of fresh air, a whiff of spring after a long winter. I could count on the fingers of one hand the number of serious relationships I'd had. I had a tendency to be tongue-tied and awkward around women. That's what 16 years in an all-boys Catholic school did. Very maladjusted!

I approached Pam carefully, inching my way over to her so that at last we could talk. At first, she was painfully shy. She hardly said a word and I carried on most of the conversation, talking about my two favorite subjects, New York and me. She told me that her uncle owned the Sutton Place apartment. He was a well-known cabinet minister in the Martial Law administration of the Philippine government. That gave me pause. Her uncle was a favorite of Imelda Marcos, the dictator's wife, and he headed both the government's pension institution as well as Philippine Airlines.

Everything in me said this wasn't a good idea, perhaps even a betrayal of my principles. But I brushed it aside. We were two people, living in a different country, which had conferred on us new identities. We weren't tied to our pasts or our families. Besides, I was just too attracted to her to let anything get in the way. Politics was not the subject tonight. Romance was. The more we talked, the more I liked her. She seemed like she enjoyed listening to my stories. There were connections between us too—she'd spent a year at the Ateneo, my old school, after it went co-ed, but had fled it for an all-girls school because, coming from the province, she had felt out of place with the mostly Manila crowd.

The party lasted till three in the morning, and I made sure to get her phone number. That very night, I began to entertain the thought that maybe I should marry her. Long ago, I decided to postpone marriage. I decided all the way back in high school that career came first, that I needed to become financially self-sufficient and only then would I look for a mate. I didn't want to be saddled down like so many of my friends with kids and a mortgage. Yet I'd been alone for so long. I was 32 now. She was ten years younger which seemed about right. My father was around nine years older than my mother. And their marriage had worked out great. She was from the Philippines too, and I figured that marriage was hard enough without the issue of a different culture coming between us.

For perhaps the first time in my life, I actually wanted to marry someone. I'd never been in this situation before. I asked myself, "Do you really want to do this?" And I answered "Yes" with all my heart. I longed to bid goodbye to a life of isolation and nights gorging on TV. In my head ran the lyrics from the song "Some Enchanted Evening" from the musical *South Pacific*: "Once you have found her, never let her go… Or all through your life you may dream all alone." I didn't want to lose her. So I planned my campaign carefully. I decided to approach this courtship differently from all my others. I flirted with her cousin at first, hoping that she'd get jealous. Maybe it would stoke her interest in me. Then I made my move.

Our first date was lunch in Central Park, that lush piece of greenery in the center of the city, with lakes, a meadow, rocks, a zoo and weedy hideaways that gave tired New Yorkers a chance to take a break from the confusion and mayhem of urban life. In those years, though, it was a dangerous place to hang around once the sun set. I had arrived early, so I bought a hot dog and a can of soda. Then I sat down and made myself comfortable on the grass, soaking in the sun and watching the people stroll by. When she reached our meeting spot, I asked her if she wanted the same thing and she said sure. So I took her over to the hot dog stand. She waited, looking at me expectantly. I waited too, munching hungrily on my hot dog, curious to see what would happen. Finally, with an exasperated shrug, she bought herself one.

I would normally have paid for her lunch, but I was a frugal guy, and she was late. I already had my sandwich. This was our first date though and for most guys, especially Filipinos, paying would have been a must. Years later, she told me that she was shocked that I hadn't paid for lunch on that first date. "But I told myself, this guy is different. He's not trying to impress me."

I like to think that we saw each other like two characters in a Broadway musical with New York as our stage. I shared my passion for movies with her.

We queued up with all the other cinema lovers at a midtown theater to watch a remastered copy of *Lawrence of Arabia*. I didn't have much money, so I took Pam to all the free or inexpensive events that I enjoyed so much. We lined up at the TKTS booth in Times Square for half-price theater tickets or whiled away entire days waiting in line to get free passes to watch Shakespeare in the Park productions. While we were standing around, we enjoyed watching a jolly prankster dressed up as a clown. He kept us all entertained with jokes or tricks as we waited, and everyone gratefully forked over a dollar or two. He was part of the experience, and we were sad when I read in *The Times* that he was one of the passengers on the TWA flight that exploded over Lockerbee, Scotland in December 1987.

Twice a year, the New York Philharmonic held free concerts in Central Park. Pam and I packed some cheese, tuna salad, crackers and wine and spread out a blanket on the Great Lawn and listened to the celestial music along with thousands of other New Yorkers. She beamed at me with what looked like pure delight, her hair hanging loosely about her neck. I leaned back with a glass of wine, stared up at the night sky, held on to her hand and thought, "This is good."

Some days, we'd sit out on the balcony of her uncle's apartment and, while sipping wine and watching the ships slip by, I'd croon the words of "Moon River" to her: "Two drifters off to see the world; there's such a lot of world to see."

"I'm not a drifter," she'd reproach me.

When you're Filipino, you know you're in a serious relationship when you start going to Sunday Mass together, which is what we began doing. It was as much a social thing as anything religious. Though with Pam, it was different. She had a deep-seated faith in God, and it was one of the things I admired in her. I was getting closer to asking for a commitment that meant living the rest of my life with this one person.

But whatever I may have believed back then, work was destined to always be a part of our life together, like an uninvited guest in our marital bed.

10 – "GOD, I LOVE THIS BUSINESS"

It was late at night. Half-eaten sandwiches and empty pizza boxes lay strewn about the law offices of Paul, Weiss, Rifkind, Wharton & Garrison, a prominent New York law firm where Reg first got a job, and which TLC Group now had on retainer. Dozens of lawyers, accountants and investment bankers had descended on the scene and were hard at work. There were people from Spain, Australia, Canada and other parts of the Beatrice International empire. Everyone had been working for two days straight.

The entire cast occupied two whole floors with several large conference rooms that were much nicer than Lewis & Clarkson's. Individual offices of the lawyers lined the walls. Plush seats and heavy wooden desks made from reddish brown mahogany wood murmured about power and expensive fees. Panels of law books stood at attention against the walls and ornate lamps hung from the ceilings. For the TLC Group team, it was the most fascinating experience of their lives and they felt happy to be part of the circus.

TLC was trying to close several transactions connected to the Beatrice International deal at once. One room hosted the negotiations on the sale of Beatrice's companies in Australia. A second room focused on the sale of its assets in Canada. Yet a third office dealt with the Beatrice companies in Spain, with the exception of its ice cream firm, which Reg wanted to hold on to. Piles of documents were stacked up in every room. Charles Clarkson, who was the Corporate Secretary for all 64 companies that were part of Beatrice International, busied himself signing hundreds of legal papers. The group dealing with the actual bid for Beatrice International met in a conference room while Reg himself commandeered one lawyer's office.

With what sounded like a thunderclap, a voice on the intercom sliced through the commotion.

"Listen up, everyone!"

People paused at whatever they were doing. It was Reg.

"The Beatrice deal has to close along with the side transactions. Each part is important because if one piece doesn't work, it all falls apart. So, concentrate. Execute. Otherwise, it will all have been for nothing. Keep cranking the numbers. Let's get Australia, Canada and Spain sold, and let's come up with our final offer for Beatrice."

As always, Reg was in command.

"We're going to fucking win this thing!"

A ragged cheer resounded through the offices. Then people went back to work, and the general hubbub resumed. Everyone was caught up in the excitement.

Reg lit up his Cuban cigar, a Monte Cristo, and walked into one room packed with Australians and our lawyers.

"All right, guys; where are we?"

A short, nervous man answered.

"As you know, Reg, we're very interested in purchasing the Beatrice operations in Australia. We understand your need for speed. And we're prepared to move quickly."

"How much are you prepared to pay for that privilege?"

"Ninety million American dollars."

Reg blew concentric circles of smoke as he puffed on his cigar. "You'll need to do better than that, boys."

"Exactly how much better?"

Reg thought for a second. "Another $10 million should do it."

The Australian executive coughed as the smoke swam around him and then looked at his colleagues. This was going to be a long night.

"What if I say no? What if I say $90 million is plenty? What if I say that I know you need this deal in order to close the Beatrice transaction?" the Australian said.

"I'd say you've come a long way for nothing." Reg took another puff on his cigar, stood up and started heading for the door, a cloud of smoke trailing him.

"Now wait a minute, Reg. There's no need for theatrics. We want the business."

"And it's a great business. There are plenty of other buyers."

Again, the Australian glanced at his compatriots. Small circles of sweat were visible in his armpits. They all looked nervous now. Finally, he turned back to Reg.

"All right," he said with a note of resignation. "$100 million it is. Naturally, we'd like some protection. This sale is going to need the approval of several governments. It may take a while. We'd like a guarantee that the terms we've agreed on today will be the same as when the deal closes."

Reg took yet another puff on his cigar and blew more circles of smoke. The room wasn't that large and the fumes from his Monte Cristo filled the air.

"Forget it," Reg said. "No guarantees. That's not the way I do business."

"It only seems fair, Mr. Lewis," a second taller Australian chimed in, a fleck of saliva staining his lips.

"Yes, but life is unfair, as Jack Kennedy said. And another thing: let's tack on an extra one million dollars to the price because of this delay. Make it $101 million."

The Australians looked aghast.

But Reg was undeterred. "This is a take-it-or-leave-it deal, boys. So, what's it going to be?"

"What about due diligence? Surely, we're going to be able to tour the plants?" the tall Aussie pleaded.

"You'll get all the relevant documents. But no one's going to go snooping around. That wouldn't be good for the employees' morale."

"But to commit to pay $100 million . . . ."

"$101 million," Reg interrupted.

"Whatever. To pay all that money without even getting the chance to kick the tires on this thing, well, frankly that's outrageous." The first guy tugged at his tie, which had a food stain on it.

"No guarantees and no due diligence. Do we have a deal?"

The guy was right. Unless Reg could close the Australian deal, the entire Beatrice transaction would collapse. Reg was taking a chance. But was he going too far?

There were a few seconds of silence.

"Yes," one of them finally said, "you have a deal."

Reg turned around and walked out, murmuring under his breath, "God, I love this business."

11 – NOBODY KNOWS WHO THE HELL YOU ARE

Reg entered the conference room where the TLC Group team was hunkered down. "OK, guys; what's the latest update?"

"We're still at 950, Reg, assuming we close Australia, Canada and Spain," said Cleve, his brow furrowed and his eyes bloodshot from lack of sleep. "We need to get all three deals over the finish line."

"We'd fucking better get all three deals done, because otherwise the Beatrice bid doesn't happen."

"Yes, Reg," they answered in unison, except for Cleve, who was silent.

"Sometimes we have to go in whether we're prepared or not," Reg said. "It's ready, fire, aim. We can't win if we're not in the game."

The boys from TLC filed into another conference room and huddled around a single black landline phone which was on speaker mode. Nobody was smiling. They looked grim. The finance, tax and accounting guys were arguing among themselves. Charles sat silent; his lips pursed.

Suddenly Reg shouted, "Shut up, guys! The auction is starting."

A voice came on suddenly. "Good evening, this is Salomon Brothers. TLC Group, what is your offer?"

Reg stared pensively into space while the world waited. Again, the faceless voice on the speakerphone spoke up. "TLC Group, what is your offer?"

All the months of hard work and haggling came down to this moment. All the faces turned to the man who was going to make the big decision. Finally, Reg declared, "This is Reginald Lewis, CEO of TLC Group. We bid $950 million."

TLC was staring over the edge of a precipice but there was no backing out.

"Thank you, Mr. Lewis," the voice said. "We will get back to you."

"All right, everybody," Reg said, "hit the phones. We need intelligence. Anything we can pick up on what the other bids are. We know the French are bidding. We know Citicorp is bidding. And who knows who the hell else is out there. Check with your sources and let's regroup before the second round of bids."

Everyone scattered to various desks. They picked up their phones from their cradles to call people. Reg himself was on the phone constantly, no sooner finishing one call than hanging up to call someone else.

An hour later, the team regrouped in the conference room.

"What have you heard?" Reg asked, staring around the room with a fierce look.

"Not much Reg," Everett admitted. "Nobody's talking."

"That's right, Reg," Cleve said. "It feels like we're going around in circles."

"We need to decide soon," Reg said as he looked around the room. "Are we going to stay at 950 million or move up?"

"I think we're good at 950," Cleve argued. "My computer model shows that should nail the deal."

"That's right," Everett agreed. "I don't think there's any room to go higher."

"I know that we're pretty much at the edge of the envelope. But let's look at what we know," Reg declared. "We know we've got Drexel in our pocket. That means $500 million if we need it. We know that we are close to getting Canada, Australia and Pedro Ballve's meat company in Spain sold, which takes the pressure off of raising the whole amount of our bid."

"By the way, remind me to fire that Beatrice manager of the Spanish operations. If a guy can't find a restaurant, he's no good at running a company." It was some executive from Beatrice management who Reg had met when touring a plant in Spain.

"I think we should move it up ... to 985 million dollars," Reg said. He was willing to bet everything to win Beatrice International. This was his moment and he would not let it pass.

"But we could just be bidding against ourselves if we go any higher," Cleve said. "How do we know there's anyone bidding even close to our price?"

"This is for all the marbles," Reg said. "I'd rather overbid than fail. If we win, we can always tinker around with the operations. See what we can fix and improve. If we lose, we're done. And we can't afford that. I've poured everything into this deal. With no intel though, it's like we're fucking guessing."

Just then, the phone rang. Everyone leaned forward in their chairs. Reg put it on speaker again.

"Hello, TLC Group," the same voice said in a tone devoid of emotion, like he was reading the phone book. "We've started the second round of bids for Beatrice International. Would you care to increase your offer?"

Reg looked at the faces clustered around him as if searching for an answer. No one said a word. What else was there to say? People could see that he was struggling with himself. He badly wanted Beatrice but how much should he bid? How much would take the deal? The team had done the math. TLC was at the outer limits of what they could comfortably offer. Go any higher and it was going to be tricky. The deal was so close that one could almost read the headline in the paper. Victory was there, staring them in the face.

Or was it bankruptcy?

Reg was quiet for a second longer and then he declared, "In for a penny, in for a pound. TLC Group bids $985 million."

Almost a billion dollars. They all squirmed a little, but Reg didn't move a muscle and kept his gaze squarely on the phone. Everyone was quiet, knowing their collective fates hung in the balance.

The voice on the phone went silent for what seemed like a very long time. Then they distinctly heard whispering in the background. They couldn't make out what was being said. Finally, the voice came back on.

"OK, TLC Group. You have the highest offer and therefore have won the bidding. There's just one problem. Nobody knows who the hell you are."

It felt like a punch in the gut. Had it all been for nothing?

At that, Reg spoke up. "We're a boutique investment shop. We did the McCall Pattern buyout just last month. You may have read about it in the *New York Times*. And we've got the backing of Drexel Burnham for our bid."

All was quiet again.

"Drexel?" the voice said. "OK. I'm assuming you've got one of those 'highly confident' letters from Milken? If so, please send it to us along with any other supporting documents you have for your bid. Thank you, gentlemen, and congratulations. You've just bought yourselves a great company."

With that, whoever it was hung up.

The TLC team looked at one another for a moment. Then they cheered in relief as much as triumph. They began to shake Reg's hand and backslap each other.

"Excellent job, everyone," Reg pronounced gleefully. "Let's head for the Harvard Club and celebrate!"

He was as happy as anyone had ever seen him. The Harvard Club in Midtown was one of Reg's favorite haunts. He knew all the waiters there.

They rode down the elevator and strode out onto the street, marching like an army, Reg in the lead, his hands in his pockets, the others struggling to keep up. A breeze from the East River washed over their faces and the aroma of freshly barbecued shish kebab from a nearby food cart wafted past. Following behind at a discreet distance was Reg's ever-present blue Bentley with John Baffoe, his Ghanian driver at the wheel.

Suddenly Reg turned to us and asked, "Is anybody looking?"

They glanced around. Nobody seemed to be paying the slightest attention. Then, without waiting for an answer, Reg jumped up in the air, kicked his heels together and let out a wild laugh. And they knew it was going to be all right and started laughing along with him. It had all happened so fast that they felt themselves getting carried along on some giant wave.

12 – MY CUP RUNNETH OVER

Over the years living in New York, during the holiday season, Pam and I would stop by one of the vendors selling Christmas trees on the street. They drove down from Vermont or Canada in their vans to sell Douglas firs, spruce, or white pine trees. The sellers always seemed to wear big smiles. She and I would pick one out—not too tall, not too bushy—and carry it back on foot through the streets to our apartment. She lugged one end, I the other. This was one of the nicer things about living in the U.S. You could buy real Christmas trees and occasionally witness a white Christmas with snow, something totally foreign in a tropical climate like the Philippines.

My birthday was on December 21, which added to the festivity of the holidays. During one of my birthdays, I walked in the door and beheld a sight that I'd never forget. Hanging from the ceiling was a forest of faxes, dangling from strings tied to the ceiling. Pam looked at me with a big smile and yelled "Surprise!" I could only stare at the faxes with my mouth open in amazement. I had no idea what was on the faxes or who they were from.

"Why don't you read them?" she suggested. I dropped my briefcase and began to examine each one. On each was a note wishing me Happy Birthday. My sisters, brother and parents sent a fax. There was a fax from Chris Atkins and one from Harold Burson. I wondered how she'd gotten him to send me a birthday fax! Then I reached for the last one and on it was a birthday greeting from the President of the United States! I couldn't believe it and asked her how in the world she was able to get a note from the president.

"Simple," she said. "I called the White House and asked them if they could send a birthday greeting for my husband. It turns out there's an office that handles those things." Both of us laughed in delight. I was impressed. Pam could do anything once she set her mind to it. I embraced her with gratitude and told myself I was the luckiest man in the world. There was just the two of us in that room with a blizzard of faxes, singing "Happy Birthday," alone and yet together in a new land. I blew out my candles on the birthday cake and made a wish. Then I pulled Pam closer and kissed her.

My parents visited us in the U.S. as often as they could afford, once a year even. I suspect they spent much of their money on those trips. Once, they even took a Greyhound bus all the way from Los Angeles to New York. Dad wanted to see the country and he always got along with his fellow travelers. He was the kind of guy who struck up conversations with strangers. He enjoyed talking to people and they, in turn, either out of politeness or genuine interest, listened to his stories.

"It's fun chatting with Americans," he'd tell us.

"It's all right when you say you're visiting from the Philippines. But Joe, their faces change when you tell them you're an American," said Mom. He waved her off.

When I was tapped for the job in New York, that was heaven for my Dad. Me, living and working in the city, doing PR—that made him as proud as anything and he liked bragging to people back home about how well I was doing.

"There's just one thing," he told me and gestured at my somewhat ramshackle studio. "You have to get a better apartment. This won't do."

I nodded my head. As it turned out, I was just getting started and poised for a takeoff.

One day, Dad was sitting in his pajamas, and he looked up from his morning paper and said, "Hijo, why don't you try to get me an article in the paper? Call some reporter, tell him my story about being in the war and maybe we can get free tickets to a Yankees game."

"You really think that would work?"

I wound up cold calling a *Daily News* sports columnist, Michael Katz. I told him about Dad's war experiences and his being a lifelong Yankee fan.

He listened for a while, then said, "Not bad, not bad."

Katz visited us in my cramped apartment to interview him.

Dad began his story. "'Must tell Mrs. Meily that her son Joe was sighted alive along with everyone else on the day of the surrender.' That's from the diary of my friend, Philip Buencamino. That's how my mother found out I'd survived the battle of Bataan. She waited outside the prison camp every day until she'd see me and then she'd toss me food over the barbed wire fence. Without that food, I'd have died there." My father's eyes gleamed as he spoke.

His voice took on an animated tone. He loved narrating tales, and this was a good one.

"After a year and a half, I was sick with dysentery. I guess I was too much of a burden for the Japs and they let me go. I spent the rest of the war picking up balls for Japanese businessmen playing tennis. Some friends asked me to join a guerrilla unit, but I told them I'd done enough and since I was the eldest of nine children, I was responsible for getting them and my parents through the war."

I watched the conversation, soaking it all up, knowing I'd made my father happy.

"Nine kids? No kidding," said Katz. "Do you ever think much about your friends, the ones that didn't make it back?"

"Not a single day goes by that I don't think about those boys that died there. Getting shot and bombed. The kids defending Lingayen Beach where the Japanese first landed, that was murder. They just weren't ready." He was silent for a time.

"I had a great time after the war though," he perked up. "The U.S. Army flew a bunch of us officers over to the States for training. I'd go to nightclubs in New York and whenever people saw my uniform, the maître d' would motion to me to come to the head of the line."

"That must have been an exciting time."

"It was. In Washington, they had these segregated buses, and all of my fellow Filipino officers were telling me, 'Joe, let's sit in the back with the colored people. We don't want any trouble.' 'No way,' I'd tell them. 'I'm sitting up here with everyone else.' And that's just what I did."

"That's a great story, Joe."

Katz arranged for us to get prime seats at a Yankees game along with a tour of the stadium. My Dad, proudly dressed in his best brown suit, jumped into the dugout as the Yankees were taking batting practice, picked up a bat and started swinging. He was as happy as a little boy. He waved to the Yankees' star, Dave Winfield, and shouted, "Hey, Dave!"

Winfield glanced at him and sort of gave him a half wave as he walked off the field. We got free hot dogs, Cokes, the works. But the best thing was that next morning, when I woke up and bought a copy of the *News*, there on the back page on June 9, 1986 was a whole column by Katz headlined, "Bataan to Bat Day and Always a Yank."

It was one of the best days of my life, and, I think, of Dad's. I still remember him grinning from ear to ear, as he studied the story sitting at the table of his favorite diner where we ate breakfast every morning. For one day, he was king of New York City, and he ambled around, watching people as they read the *Daily News* or bought a copy from newsstands. There's no better feeling in the world than to have your story spread out on a whole page of the paper and know people are reading about you. I knew that from my work in public relations, but this was the first time it felt so personal for me.

I wound up Xeroxing—that's what we used to call it — copies of the article and putting one on everyone's desk at the PR agency. I overheard one of the girls referring to me, saying, "I thought you said he was shy?" Her friend just shrugged.

When it came time for him and Mom to leave for Manila, Dad moped around. "Ay naku, hijo," he'd tell me in the vernacular. "We have to go home now."

"Do you think I should return to Manila?"

"Of course not! Don't you dare."

"Even if I got a job as a high-level executive in some big company?"

"Forget it. You'd still be like everyone else there. Stuck in traffic."

He told me that his dream was to retire in the U.S. and he and my mother would watch the Yankees and follow them on the road from city to city. That sounded like a fine idea, I told him. But he never did get to live out that fantasy. My father had many great ideas, like doing a husband-and-wife radio talk show doling out marital advice to couples in California. At the time, I thought it far-fetched but looking at how talk radio has developed, I now think he was ahead of his time. I could picture my father being some kind of radio personality railing against politicians or maybe he and Mom could listen sympathetically to sob stories from listeners and give soothing words of advice. In any case, he wound up getting stuck in the Philippines, daydreaming about following the Yankees around the U.S.

I introduced them to Pam with some apprehension. They seemed to get along and she did her best to take care of them. She planned trips that we took all over the East Coast—to Maine to sample lobsters, then to Pennsylvania—where Dad, who was always spunky, grabbed my mother and ushered her to the dance floor at an outdoor concert. With everyone watching and a full moon in the night sky, they started to sway to a Cole Porter tune, "Begin the Beguine."

One day, Mom and Dad talked to me about Pam. "She seems like a nice girl, hijo. But couldn't you get one of these 'Americanitas?'" he said, referring to the locals.

I was surprised by his question but figured that he wanted me to truly become an American and be part of life here in every way. I explained to him that it was hard to meet college girls, those I could actually talk to and that marriage to a Filipina might be easier because we had more in common.

"You do what you want, Butch. I'm sure you'll make the right choice. But you're the kind of person who needs to be married." My mother was always supportive.

Pam learned how to cook, and she prepared dinner for us on certain nights of the week. I especially enjoyed her lasagna and Sloppy Joes. For the first time in my life, I found someone who I could really talk to and confide in. The fact that she came from Zamboanga, a city in the southern Philippines— which back then was a distant, sleepy town laden with Spanish influence and architecture—only made her more attractive to me, because I was tired of all the ultra-sophisticated Manila girls that I'd grown up with and saw her as a simpler and sweeter alternative.

I started to think, "This is it." I was getting older. Many of my friends had long since settled down. It seemed fortuitous that we'd met at that Fourth of July party I'd gatecrashed. It looked like God had somehow answered my prayers and lifted me out of my loneliness. Because I was in love, for sure. One weekend, we motored up to Bear Mountain, a nature preserve just over an hour's drive from New York City. I'd rented a cottage by a lake. The water was cold but we went swimming anyway. That night, after we made love, I finally asked her to marry me, and she said yes. My cup runneth over, I told myself.

13 – MY TURN AT BAT

Once we'd bagged Beatrice International, it was my turn at bat. The next morning, I explained to Reg our plan for announcing the deal to the press. Chris Atkins and I had worked it out carefully. I was going to break the news in just three papers: *The New York Times*, *The Wall Street Journal*, and the *Financial Times*. They were—what we called in the business—"opinion leaders," I told Reg. Once they carried the news, everyone else would follow. This way, we could control the narrative.

I arranged for interviews with Reg with a handpicked reporter from each publication. I also lined up a list of friendly sources for the reporter to talk to. These were investment bankers, lawyers and others favorably disposed to TLC Group. Jonathan Hicks from *The Times* was Black, and, in those days, it was easier to get a Black reporter to cover a Black businessman. I had to play every card I had and that included race.

"Why the *Financial Times*?" Reg asked.

"You're hanging on to the European companies and we need to start building your profile over there. The Europeans read *FT*. There'll be a lot of interest in who you are." This had been Chris' idea.

He thought for a minute, then said, "OK, but there's just one thing. I'm going to join Loida and the kids for a holiday in the south of France on Saturday so we 're going to have to do these interviews before then."

I was aghast. "You're going on vacation?"

"Sure. Don't you think I deserve one? I promised the family and I'm not going to break my promise."

He'd never before let his family stand in the way of business. I had the feeling he was doing it just because it was the opposite of what everyone else would do in his place.

"But today's Thursday!" I protested. "That means we're going to have to get everything done in the next day and a half."

"I leave on the Concorde at ten on Saturday morning. Get everything finished by then or forget it. You're going to have to put on your running shoes if you're going to keep up with me."

I was tempted to debate the matter, but I knew it was useless.

I acted speedily. I briefed each reporter, told them the story was embargoed till Monday, and had them interview our secondary sources to fill out the story. Then Jonathan and *The Wall Street Journal* reporter who was based in Chicago, Beatrice's headquarters, interviewed Reg on the phone. There was no time for face-to-face interviews. The story was set to break Monday morning.

I was running out of time, so I arranged to have the *Financial Times* reporter interview Reg in the back of his Bentley as we raced to JFK airport early Saturday morning. I was getting dizzy between Baffoe's driving, which felt like he was treating the Bentley like some kind of sports car, and trying to follow the interview between Reg and the reporter. We pulled up to the Air France Concorde terminal and somehow talked our way into the lounge where this Brit and I tried to finish the interview before Reg boarded the plane. Airport security was much more casual back then. The lounge resembled a living room, not mine but that of a rich person. We sipped champagne and munched on hors d'oeuvres as we sat in these red opulent chairs, huddled around a table and speaking in conspiratorial tones as the reporter scribbled away.

The Concorde was the ultimate experience in 1987. Movie stars and the top business leaders flew it. It took off like an ordinary airplane and waited till it was over the Atlantic before it broke the sound barrier to avoid shattering windows on the East Coast. A slight shudder was all the passengers felt as the plane zipped past Mach 2, twice the speed of sound. Passengers reached Paris in an unbelievable three and a half hours compared to the normal six-to-seven-hour flight. The next step would be flying the Concorde to Tokyo, which would bring the Philippines much closer to New York, or so I hoped.

There was a first cabin where many of the celebrities stayed and a second cabin for the rest of the people. The stewardesses lavished passengers with personal attention. Every passenger emerged with a really expensive gift like a Tiffany spoon, a tiny clock or a piece of jewelry. When I finally did get to ride the plane, more often than not, I glimpsed a movie star—Richard Gere, Jessica Lange, or even Van Johnson, who I used to watch on old movies they showed on TV in Manila: *Meet Me in St. Louis, Thirty Seconds Over Tokyo, A Guy Named Joe.*

Reg flew off. I spent the weekend helping our trio of reporters put the finishing touches to their stories. There were countless phone calls, questions that needed to be answered, facts that needed to be checked. For two days, we became the closest of friends, fellow conspirators in a plot that would rock the world. I woke up early Monday with a sense that this was going to be one of the most important days of my life. I bent low to kiss Pam goodbye.

"A kiss for luck," I told her.

She rose up, rubbed her eyes, leaned on her elbow and murmured, "Good luck. You're going to be great. I love you." Even half awake, she looked fresh and clean and smelled pleasantly of left-over perfume. She made me want to do my best for her.

"I love you, too," I answered and then hurried out the door.

New York was just waking up, and to me, it had never seemed so magical and new. The portable kiosks that sold coffee and bagels were just opening up. Commuters were beginning to file out of the subway. Store shutters were being rolled up. I bought copies of all three newspapers at the newsstand, and sat on the sidewalk, oblivious to everyone's stares. The story made the front page of the business section of *The New York Times* with a photo of Reg to boot.

Beatrice Unit Brings $985 Million – International Food Is Sold to TLC Group The TLC Group, a New York investment firm, has agreed to buy the Beatrice International Food Company from the parent of the Beatrice Companies for $985 Million, TLC officials said yesterday. (That would be Reg and me.).... *People familiar with the transaction said the management of Beatrice's international food business would have a small stake in the new company.* (This came from Reg.)

As part of his strategy, Reg agreed to give the top managers of Beatrice shares to get them to think like owners of the company instead of as mere employees. That would motivate them to push profits higher. He'd done the same thing at McCall Pattern, rewarding the two senior executives with shares of stock worth millions once the company was sold.

Both the *Financial Times* and the *Wall Street Journal* played the story up with the FT featuring Reg's photo as well. Just like that, a new star had burst on the firmament of Wall Street and Main Street.

Even the gang at TLC was impressed. Cleve laughed and gave me a high five as he told me, "My neighbor in Stamford, who has never said a word to me in all the years I've lived in our neighborhood, suddenly stopped by with a bottle of champagne after the Beatrice story."

The news swept the world like a firestorm. "Black-Owned Firm to Buy Beatrice Unit," screamed the *Washington Post*. A Black man buying a major company was news, although since Reg was acquiring Beatrice's overseas operations the practical effect on ordinary Americans was minimal. Not so with the African-American community. We got calls from all the Black papers including *Black Enterprise*, the Black business bible whose senior reporter, Alfred Edmonds, as instructed by his editor Derek Dingle, had just interviewed Reg for a story on the McCall sale before news of the Beatrice deal broke. The name of Reginald Lewis was on everyone's lips. Like the Concorde, he'd broken a barrier and if he could do it, perhaps others could smash through it as well.

As Chris and I had planned, every outlet—print, TV, radio—followed the three papers' lead and, since so little was known about Reginald Lewis and TLC Group, they were forced to rely on our backgrounders for information. Associated Press, CBS News, *Washington Post, Chicago Tribune.* Each outlet interviewed someone from our list of approved and well-briefed sources or quoted from the three original stories. It was like a painting, and I was the artist whether or not people knew it. Manipulation can be a great thing.

Public relations can be complicated but also very simple. Controlling the message is paramount. Most people may not realize it but much of what they read in the press or on websites or watch on TV starts with a PR person operating in the shadows. Everything that comes out of the White House, McDonald's, the National Football League, you name it. Hallmark Cards first popularized Valentine's Day in 1913 as a way to sell greeting cards and it can probably take the credit for the popularity of other semi-holidays, Grandparents' Day, Secretaries' Day and so on. So it was here and now with me at the helm of the news about the Beatrice deal.

The only people unhappy about the publicity were the Beatrice executives and our Burson colleagues in Chicago. The Beatrice boys were upset because we jumped the gun on the announcement. They threatened to cancel the deal, which would have been the end of me. But Reg, who was safely ensconced in the south of France, appeared unconcerned. He never even mentioned it to me. A Burson manager called me screaming about how Beatrice was their account. They should have been consulted and handled the press, not the New York office. Chris, my boss at Burson New York, protected me though, deflecting all the complaints from Burson Chicago and pronounced it "a pimple." Our plan had succeeded and everything else was pretty much beside the point.

Also unhappy was John Johnson, the now-former number one Black executive in the country who had built his publishing empire consisting of *Ebony* and *Jet* magazines the old-fashioned way. He called us up as well. I happened to be out at the time, and he reached my deputy, Jennifer Colville, a young Yale graduate.

"I am like a woman scorned," Johnson screamed at her, incandescent with rage that he had been displaced overnight from the top of the Black business pyramid. He reduced Jennifer to tears by the time he was done shouting. I was heartily sorry that I hadn't spoken to him instead of poor Jennifer, because I was pretty sure that I could have handled him, even in his rage, one way or the other. It was completely unexpected as well, since we were making no claims as to who was the top African-American businessman in the country. We were only concerned with getting Reg and his Beatrice triumph out in the media. But there was no stopping us now.

From then on, I went everywhere with Reg. We tramped the factory floors of the potato chip company in Ireland and gave speeches to baffled employees in warehouses in France, who had never before had a CEO speak directly to them and shake their hands, much less a Black CEO from New York who spoke to them through an interpreter. Reg brought a uniquely American style to the running of what was now known as TLC Beatrice International. He liked meeting his new employees and he wanted them to like him. We sampled the products of each of the ice cream firms in seven countries. He'd ask me from time to time, "How do I look?" as he preened about in his dapper dark suit with a blue shirt and a red tie.

"You look good," I'd say.

"We're not shooting for good," he admonished me. "We're shooting for great."

All this time, I was billing him by the hour, and it was adding up. One day, Chris dragged me along to a meeting with Reg and had me wait outside Reg's office while he had a closed door, one on one with him. As I sat in a swivel chair, I could hear plenty of shouting and looked at Deidra, Reg's secretary. She kept typing away, ignoring the whole thing as though it happened all the time.

A little later, Chris emerged looking shaken. We walked out of TLC onto Wall Street. It was raining and we took a cab back to Burson. Drops of water trickled down his face as Chris mumbled something. He looked like he'd staggered out of a boxing match. From the yelling, I thought Reg had fired Burson.

Getting money out of Reg was never easy. Chris had taken Reg on, one on one. Later, I would see Reg break off lifelong friendships over the issue of paying fees. It took me a while before I understood what he was saying: "We got paid.... And we also got a six-figure bonus for Burson." I turned and looked at him with my mouth open and a wide grin on my face. So this was what success looked like.

14 – "I COULD NO LONGER LOOK AT THEM WITH SELF-RESPECT"

Pam and I were married in December 1987. Because of my work on the Reg Lewis account, Burson paid for our honeymoon in the Philippines. My Dad, ever the showman, arranged for Pam to ride on a horse-drawn carriage, a "calesa" in the local lingo, up to the church doors where little girls tossed petals of "sampaguitas," fragrant white jasmine flowers, at her. I felt like it was raining not flowers, but stars.

Then one morning in 1988, less than a year after the acquisition of Beatrice International, Reg called me over for a meeting. He sat in a chair behind the desk in his office with his fists perched under his chin and bade me to sit down.

"We're paying Burson a lot of money to have you tagging along with me," he started. "I was thinking that we'd probably save money if we just hired you full-time. What do you think?"

I was pleasantly surprised and fumbled for an answer when he stopped me cold.

"We'll double your salary plus there'll be bonuses and stock options."

At the time, Burson was paying me $50,000 a year. That meant crashing through the $100,000 ceiling! Did I hear bonuses and stock options? Now this truly was the American Dream. I didn't need any time to think about it. I jumped up, shook his hand and accepted on the spot.

Pam was ecstatic, her eyes wide with delight. "Oh my God, it's really happening," she said. These were exciting times for both of us. It looked like the fulfillment of all my hopes and dreams for a good life. I had come to America just 11 years ago with not much in my pocket and here I was getting a princely salary plus a yearly bonus of maybe $50,000 to $150,000 and what I viewed as the path to true wealth: stock options in the company which I could later sell for many times their initial value. I could never have done as well back home where, at the time, people were happy with a regular salary of maybe $6,000 a year and a couple of weeks off. I was a long way from where I'd started on the smoky, traffic-clogged arteries of Manila.

When he heard the news, Chris congratulated me, though he looked worried. "I think it's too soon," he said. "You've still got a lot to learn. But that's the way it goes in an agency. Some of the best people wind up working with their clients."

He did make a point of seeing Reg one more time. "You're getting a good man, Reg," Chris told him. "There's just one thing that Harold Burson asked me to pass on to you."

"Yeah, what's that?"

"If you ever intimidate him so much that he can't tell you the truth, he'll be useless to you."

Reg said nothing, but he looked thoughtful. I mulled that advice over.

Later, Chris pulled me aside and whispered, "I don't mean that you should commit suicide. Choose your moments. But try to give him your honest and best advice."

Chris was nothing if not sensible. All the time I was with Reg and with the other chieftains who followed him, I tried my best to live up to that credo, if not always successfully.

There were casualties though. The glow of the Beatrice transaction was lost on some, particularly Cleve Christophe. "There'd been a lot of ranting and raving," Cleve told me later. "I think Reg thought there was no way I would leave with all this money on the table after the Beatrice deal. Then one morning before the Beatrice deal was completed, after having endured yet another tirade from Reg, I was shaving, and I looked myself in the mirror and my throat caught as I said, 'I can no longer look at my wife and two kids with self-respect if I'm willing to accept this shit for money.' Then and there I knew it was over. I did not want to jeopardize the deal by quitting; but I vowed that after it was done, I would be done."

One morning, soon after the closing of the Beatrice transaction, Reg and Cleve had it out one last time and Cleve described the scene for me. They were coatless and wearing their shirts and ties. They confronted each other like boxers in Reg's corner office. Reg's arms hung loosely at his side, his fists clenched, with his back to his desk. His face was flushed, and his eyes had an eerie glare to them.

"It's no use, Reg. I've made up my mind to go."

"But why now? Things are going well. We've got Beatrice and there will be other deals. After all the years of fighting, we've won."

"You've won. The rest of us were just along for the ride."

"Everyone did pretty well from what I recall. You got a six-figure bonus."

"That's chump change. You said I'd get equity."

"And someday you will. But as you know, your employment agreement states that it's at the option of the chairman. Is that what this is about?"

"Not just that, no."

"Is it the shouting and the cursing? I plan to change all that. Things are going to be different around here from now on."

"I just think it's time for me to go. I want to start my own firm. Do my own deals."

"And there's nothing I can do to change your mind? We've come a long way together, Cleve."

Cleve shook his head.

Reg's mood changed. "What the hell? If you're intent on committing economic suicide, I'm not going to stand in your way. When do you want to leave?"

"I don't want to do anything disruptive."

"Don't do me any favors."

Cleve started to walk out the door. Then Reg called out to him.

"We used to be friends, Cleve."

"And your friend joined you as your partner. Then I became your employee, Reg."

With that, Cleve strode out of the office.

As one of Reg's oldest friends left him for good, he stood alone, just him and the furniture. He looked angry but also forlorn. Cleve was one of the few guys I knew who left TLC Group with his dignity intact.

Later, I heard that Reg had a change of heart and actually tried to get Cleve to come back. On Cleve's last day, Reg took the trouble to take him in his car to catch his train to Connecticut at Grand Central Station and even told him that he "had the makings of an entrepreneur."

"Reg kinda screwed Cleve," one of the staff told me. "The thing about Reg was that he wanted it all. So there wasn't much left for anyone else."

I began to wonder if I'd made the right choice leaving Burson to be part of TLC Beatrice. I was beginning to see more flashes of Reg's temperament, his raging and cursing. The curtain was being pulled back.

But for now, the money made it worth it, or so I believed.

Joining TLC Beatrice International put me in a whole new league financially. I earned more money than I'd ever dreamed of and soon purchased a Manhattan condo in the Waterford, a new building on Second Avenue and 93rd Street, and, years later, a country home in the quaint town of Woodstock in the Catskills in upstate New York. There was one year where I booked a million dollars.

I had reached the top of the ladder. For an immigrant from the Philippines who used to pay $287 a month for his rent-controlled, cockroach-filled New York City "garden" apartment, it was exhilarating. At 34, I had scaled the heights of my profession and made it in America. I was playing in a much bigger arena now. And I had done it on my own. At that instant, I stood on the cusp of a new phase of my life, flushed with excitement and dreams of fortune.

15 – HE'S A "PARVENU"

Soon after I joined Beatrice in 1988, I moved to Paris, spending months at a time there and leaving Pam alone in New York to fend for herself. She was working as an interior designer and couldn't join me very often. Years before, I had taken French classes at Alliance Francaise. I never imagined that someday I'd get a chance to live in the city whose very name invoked romance and beauty. Shortly after the Beatrice acquisition, Reg, Loida and their two daughters relocated to the French capital. As always, Reg wanted the best. The family rented a spacious apartment overlooking the Place du Palais Bourbon, which ran straight into the *Assemblee Nationale* and, as a result, there were always armed soldiers on the street. It was an exquisite setting, featuring ornate chairs, elegant couches with decorative patterns painted on them and chiseled desks that looked like they came straight from the houses of the old pre-French Revolution aristocracy. Chandeliers hung above the living room and dinner table. It was like a page from a book on French royalty. Classic and classy.

The Lewises hosted a number of parties, and like everything else, Reg made sure that things were perfect down to the last detail. We pored over the seating charts; we checked the wine. The slightest mistake triggered a flood of expletives and added to the growing pressure on me. I felt like I was walking on eggshells whenever I was around him.

Occasionally, we flew Beatrice International's board members and their wives over on the Concorde for a meeting. Loida and Reg also hosted parties for the managers of the Beatrice companies in Europe. The Palais du Bourbon apartment put on its best face for the festivities and created an immediate impression on all who entered. The view from its windows of the street below and the *Assemblee Nationale* never failed to enthrall. Tables for eight or ten were spread about the living room. Waiters scooted about, precariously balancing trays of champagne or canapes. Jean Pierre Tegnet, Reg's personal assistant from the Ivory Coast, oversaw everything with a critical eye along with the French chef, Patrick, and of course, me.

Husband and wife greeted everyone as they entered. Loida, in particular, moved among the guests with ease. She learned French in her spare time and knew some Spanish, which isn't that different from Italian, so she could pretty much converse with everyone. I was surprised at the degree of knowledge about our operations she displayed. There was Sanson of our Italian ice cream company, a bitter old man unhappy with life who feuded with us constantly; Pedro Massenet, the bright young manager of La Menorquina ice cream in Spain; and Vincent O'Sullivan, the cheerful, ever-ebullient head man of Tayto, our profitable potato chip company in Ireland.

Every now and then, after all the guests had gone home, I'd spot Reg standing alone at the large window looking out at the street below. He was in a tux because Reg and Loida's parties were always black tie. He'd be drinking Dom Pérignon champagne and puffing on his Cuban cigar. A cloud of smoke swirled around him. Then, for no apparent reason, he'd smile.

With all the good things that were happening however, I never got the feeling that Reg was ever truly happy. No matter how much money he made, he always seemed isolated, apart from everyone. None of his old friends came around nor did he seem to have anyone who was really close to him except for the people on his payroll. Those moments by the window were some of the few times when I thought he was genuinely happy.

Everyone else from TLC Group stayed in New York, although they made frequent trips to Paris for work. Reg lightened up in Paris. He smiled more often and told more jokes. He was much easier to get along with than in New York. He confided that he felt there was less discrimination there than in the U.S.

"I get a headache every time I have to go back to New York," he shared with me. It was true that the stress level went way up when we were back in the city.

Some evenings in Europe when we were traveling, I'd hurry downstairs to the hotel's restaurant before Reg and Loida came down to dinner. I always tried to stay one step ahead of him to avoid arguments. I started by handing out money to everyone. I told them, "My boss and his wife are coming down for dinner. We'd like your best table and the service has to be perfect."

"Of course, Monsieur," the maître d' said as he handed me back the cash. "But there's no need for this really. We haven't even started serving."

"Keep it," I insisted. "Just please take care of them."

I picked out a table on the side because I thought they might want privacy. It was hard guessing what Reg preferred. Some nights, he wanted a table in the center of the room where everyone could see them and other nights, he preferred discretion.

We fostered a close relationship with the French banks. Elie Souaf, a white-haired French Middle Eastern Arab who wore expensive suits, was a regular guest. As were Remmert Laan and Osman Mardin of Lazard Freres, the prestigious global investment bank. Remmert was a French aristocrat who was always immaculately dressed and hunted on weekends while Osman was Turkish but had studied at Cambridge and Harvard Business School and landed a job at Lazard.

Remmert was snooty with us, which seemed to be a French national trait, and Reg could sense it. One time, he asked me to call him.

"What for?"

"Just ask him what he really thinks of me. But do it in such a way that he won't think you'll tell me."

"How the hell can I do that? Besides, I don't think that's a good idea."

"Do it. And what's more, I'm going to listen in."

"You've got to be kidding? I can't do that. It's going to be awkward, and it's not really kosher. How about if I just call him and report back to you?"

"Who do you work for Butch? Him or me?"

I couldn't believe that Reg was actually asking me to commit this subterfuge. I didn't particularly like Remmert but I knew instinctively this was wrong. I could sense Reg was testing me to see how far he could push me. In the end, he was my boss, and I held my tongue.

"Just remember that. Now go ahead."

"All right, but you gotta keep quiet."

I reluctantly dialed Remmert and started chatting away while Reg listened in on an extension. It felt like a spying expedition. My heart beat a little faster. I was uneasy but gently began to probe into just what he really thought of our great leader. He was surprisingly candid. "He's a bit of a—how shall I say it? —a 'parvenu.' You know what that means? A newcomer, a social climber."

All of a sudden, we heard this voice thundering on the line. "You motherfucker! Who the hell do you think you are? I'm going to fire Lazard!"

Remmert was dumbfounded. "What? Who is that?"

I was too embarrassed by the deception and my role in it to utter a thing.

He began to grasp the situation and stumblingly tried to explain. "Mr. Lewis? I think there's been some misunderstanding."

We never did fire Lazard. In fact, we continued to do business with Remmert, though we started seeing a whole lot more of Osman and a lot less of Remmert after that call. The whole stunt left a sour taste in my mouth, and it certainly cost me any credibility I had with Remmert and Lazard. I sensed that all this success was changing Reg, enlarging his horizons but also giving him a bigger ego. He was pushing boundaries. Yet there were those stock options and six-figure annual bonuses to think of. I knew that I needed what they refer to as F U money to leave. So I stayed on.

There were other distractions in Paris. Reg took these long, languid, very European lunches with several courses and wine in these elegant restaurants where waiters were stylishly attired in bow ties and black coats. Then he smoked his Cuban cigars. Afterwards we strolled down the avenues and prowled the art galleries accompanied by Jean-Jacques Dutko, Reg's favorite art dealer, and Jean Pierre.

There is an old saying in France that no man is a hero to his valet. I guess that applied to Jean Pierre and his relationship with Reg though Jean Pierre was his personal assistant and not his valet. He was Reg's all-around man, tending to his every need whether cigars or making the arrangements for parties. He had a background in accounting and scrutinized all the bills and the work product of Reg's secretary. He didn't finish college though because Reg had recruited him while he was still a student.

"I'm going to make you an offer that you can't refuse," Reg told Jean Pierre in the TLC office in New York City one day before asking him to move to Paris and offering him a princely salary. "I've just bought Beatrice International. The European headquarters is going to be in Paris and I'm going to be moving there with the family. You know the language. You know the culture. You'll be very useful."

Aside from Reg's family, Jean Pierre was the first person to see Reg in the morning before going to work and he was often the last person to see him at his home at night. If I was close to Reg, Jean Pierre was even closer. He got to see the man behind the screen. When the TLC gang would see him in the morning, they'd ask him one question and it wasn't about the weather. "How is Mr. Lewis this morning?" The answer to that question in New York or Paris determined how the day was going to go. If he was in a bad mood, best to shy away from him. Not a good time to bring up problems.

Poor Jean Pierre could never go on vacation. He always seemed to be on duty from 6:30 in the morning to 8 or 9 at night. He only got to see his wife, Esther, who was working in New York every three or four months and then only for a few days. Once he flew from Paris to New York on the Concorde on Tuesday to be with his wife and then flew back to Paris on Wednesday. He and I often hung around together, sitting under an awning at an outdoor table of one of the city's many bistros, so we could grab lunch during our rare breaks. It was a wonderful setting where we could watch all these stylish French people stroll by us. But we were too wound up and tense to enjoy ourselves. Instead, we hurriedly munched on *salad niçoise*, a dish of olives, tomatoes, anchovies, tuna and green vegetables, that Jean Pierre had introduced me to, then gulped down a double expresso. All through the meal, we commiserated with one another about the terrible life we were living in one of the most beautiful cities in the world. We complained about the boss and our forlorn, empty lives. He missed his wife, as did I, and I was glad to have someone to talk to.

Jean Pierre was under so much pressure that twice, he had to see the doctor because of heart palpitations and shortness of breath.

"You have two choices," the doctor told him. "You can stay with your boss and die of a heart attack. Or you can find another job and live."

There came a time when his wife was pregnant and about to give birth. He finally worked up the nerve to ask for a vacation. Reg said no. He left anyway and our company lawyer told him the next day not to bother to come back to work. I lost a friend. I learned later that Reg cut off his health insurance even though his wife was giving birth. However, Everett Grant, our financial person, went out on a limb and reinstated the insurance.

When the TLC guys from New York were in Paris, we'd make a point of using our expense accounts to eat at the priciest restaurants as a consolation and maybe a bit of revenge for our prolonged sojourns in this most exquisite of jails. One place we especially liked was Lucas Carton, a Michelin-rated restaurant near the Madeleine Church that had a charming art-nouveau décor. Charles Clarkson, one of the longtime TLC lawyers, would infuriate the chef by insisting on having ketchup with his steak.

"But Monsieur, it will destroy all the flavor," the chef would argue, his face turning red. But Charles being Charles, he'd demand his ketchup from the chef and the Frenchman would throw up his hands in dismay.

One night, Reg treated all of us to a film at a theater on the Champs Elysee. *Wall Street*, the movie starring Michael Douglas as a Michael Milken-like figure and Charlie Sheen as a young ingenue in an investment bank that seemed like it was modeled on Drexel Burnham, had just opened and Reg and his team including me were keen to see it. We felt a little out of place seated among the largely French audience. We were excited though as the lights dimmed and the murmur of the crowd died down. I felt that familiar feeling of anticipation and eagerness that came over me anytime I watched a movie. As the story of Gordon Gekko whose god was greed and the magic of trading in stocks and engineering take overs of companies spun out before us, I could sense the undercurrents passing between our tiny band and the characters on the screen. When it ended, Reg beamed at us in glee. He could not stop talking about it and how it seemed to mirror Milken and what we, TLC Group now TLC Beatrice International, were carrying out in Europe. We were living the movie although we certainly weren't doing anything illegal.

The art dealer, Jean-Jaques Dutko, took us to all the galleries to show Reg the latest modernist art or a Degas, Picasso, Miro, ornate Middle Eastern carpets, or ancient Roman sculptures which I was interested in because of the history.

"Bonjour, Monsieur Lewis. You're looking good." The dealers were always happy to see him. The showrooms were cozy places with all manner of art jammed next to one another.

Dutko and Reg haggled with the dealers and, more often than not, Reg ordered a piece to be delivered to his home. Then we crowded into the black Mercedes that always followed us around when we caroused about the city, with Patrick LeLongh, Reg's French driver at the wheel. I enjoyed these outings; although, like I said, we always had to be on our guard with Reg. He never let any remark that he believed to be false, mistaken, or racist pass unchallenged. If someone said it was chilly in Paris and Reg didn't agree, he would let that person know about it right then and there.

That would occasionally include our Beatrice managers. After we bought Beatrice, the Italian ice cream operator Sanson had sued us in Italy over his rights as a shareholder of the ice cream company that bore his name. I convinced Reg that the only way to deal with him was to take the fight to him in his home country. Italians were just like Filipinos. They could not stand being embarrassed. Sanson had based his reputation on his supposed ownership of the ice cream company. Once word got around that an American multinational and not his family was the real owner, he'd be finished. So we stuffed our lawyers on a plane to Milan, Italy's financial capital, and working with Burson's Italian office, staged a press conference where we essentially litigated our case before the Italian business community and the public. As I had hoped, the negative publicity put pressure on Sanson and he soon agreed to a settlement.

Then, of course, there were the Bauds, the family that ran our supermarkets in the Paris area, Franprix and LeaderPrice. They were hard-nosed businessmen, *pieds noirs,* as the French derisively termed the refugees from Algeria who'd returned home after France gave up its 130-year-old colony there in 1962.

Reg respected them because they contributed a healthy chunk of the profits of Beatrice. Once, he arranged to give Jean Baud, the patriarch of the family, a brand-new red Corvette ZR-1, while his brother Jacques got an Oldsmobile convertible. Jean Pierre arranged to import the cars to France. Reg presented the vehicles to the brothers in front of the Crillon Hotel, one of the city's grandest, where I stayed on occasion. The Crillon faced the Place de la Concorde, roughly translated as place of harmony, which is ironic considering this was where Marie Antoinette and so many others lost their heads to the guillotine during the French Revolution.

Traffic swirled around us, and curious onlookers gathered to watch. Jean and Jacques couldn't stop smiling as Reg presented each of them with the keys to their cars. The Bauds looked like little boys who'd gotten their long-awaited Christmas presents. Reg looked pleased with himself. But it didn't make any difference. Maybe they viewed our giving them the cars as a sign of weakness because relations with the family remained tough.

As for me, I stayed mostly at the Grand Hotel, which was reasonably priced and not far from our office. It soon became almost like a second home for me. The hotel was set in this 19th-century building near the Madeleine Church and the old Opera House.

I spent many nights in my room, jet-lagged and sleepless from our trips, ordering all kinds of dishes from room service in the middle of the night, like fried eggs and bacon with rice and lots of ketchup. Reg had offered me a corporate apartment, but I said no, preferring to have the services and the freedom of a hotel. I sensed that if I stayed in a company apartment, I would be even more beholden to him and under his sway and I recoiled from that prospect.

"You're the only guy I know who turned down a corporate apartment," Reg told me in amazement. I needed a break from him, and I fought to make sure that I had some down time for myself when I could do whatever I wanted; watch a movie, drink wine at a sidewalk café, whatever it was, so long as I wasn't with Reg. Those precious hours away from him kept me going. Living in an apartment that the company paid for would have left me no privacy.

Inevitably, my thoughts turned to Pam and how she was doing in New York. She couldn't join me except for brief trips because of her job. I yearned for her but I had such a close working relationship with Reg that I could never get away from Paris for long. I was young and life was exciting. But I missed Pam and longed to go home to New York. Those absences set a pattern for us because more often than not, my work and my career working with high profile bosses often took time away from my family. I didn't realize till much later that there was a price to be paid for that.

In Paris, we worked all the time. American holidays, French holidays, it didn't matter. I remember one May Day, which is a major holiday in France, when Reg insisted that we go to the office. I got there first. Our offices were on the second floor of a swanky building with a balcony looking out on 9 Rue de la Paix, which since the 1800s had been known as the street of expensive jewelry stores. There was nothing for sale that I could afford, and I never bothered to check out the merchandise. That day, I ran into a rally that was wending its way right down the Rue and I hurtled up the steps. Close on my heels was Patrick, the driver. Reg had sent him along with me to check things out because we knew the French were big on May Day demonstrations and we heard they might be marching past our office.

Patrick and I made our way to the balcony. There was a mass of people on the street, and they chanted slogans in French. They waved French flags and hoisted big banners and statues of the saints and the Virgin Mary. As a Catholic, I didn't think it was anything out of the ordinary at first. As I watched though, I began to get a sense that this was not a typical religious procession like we had back in the Philippines. People looked agitated and shouted angrily. They were mad about something. All of a sudden, they caught sight of us. They began screaming. I stepped back and asked Patrick what they were yelling.

"They're saying, 'Jews out of France,'" Patrick muttered without expression. I wondered if Patrick was Jewish, but I never asked. The degree of anti-Semitism in France surprised me. The marchers appeared to have stepped out of a painting of the Middle Ages and straight onto the Rue de la Paix. Reg had always discouraged me from making ethnic jokes of any kind.

"It's not that I don't have a sense of humor," he said. "It's just that I believe when you go down that road, it leads to the same place—where people look down on other groups because of the way they look or what they believe in. I can't stand that."

I told Reg to forget about coming to work that day. If this crowd didn't like Jews, they probably didn't like people of color either.

The novelist Ernest Hemingway wrote that if you are lucky enough to live in Paris when you are young, it stays with you the rest of your life. Because Paris, in his words, was a "moveable feast." So it was for me. No matter where else I lived or visited, and in the future, I would journey to many distant lands, my memories of Paris stayed with me and colored my view of life.

16 – SEARCHING FOR A BANANA IN VENICE

In Paris, we worked on Thanksgiving and other American holidays. Reg turned to me once and reminded me, "Do you realize that it's Thanksgiving today and we're working?" I nodded back at him silently. He smiled. It was hard on the TLC guys. They were desperate to get out of Paris and make it back home. They planned and schemed and made a mad dash to Charles de Gaulle airport most weekends or for big holidays. They were never safe though, not until they boarded the plane and it took off. Because they knew they might get a call on their cellphones, which were still new and big and clunky back then, or hear a voice on the airport speakers ordering them to return to TLC Beatrice Paris, which happened on more than one occasion.

"Calling for Monsieur Everett Grant and Monsieur Mark Thorne; please report to the Information Desk. There is an urgent telephone call for you."

"Do you hear anything, Everett?" Mark, our chief financial officer at the time, asked.

Everett grinned. "No, I don't believe so, Mark." Then they both got up and boarded the plane.

One Thanksgiving after working all day, I sat down to a sumptuous turkey dinner with the Lewis family at their Palais du' Bourbon apartment when I suddenly got a call from Pam. We'd had a fight over the phone that day just before she left for the bank near our apartment to withdraw money from an ATM machine. She felt so sad about it that she walked around looking down at the pavement, the mark of an easy prey, especially in the New York of the late '80s and early '90s. Someone grabbed her purse and, while it was still attached to her, dragged her on the ground. She was shaken up and wanted me to come home right away.

I turned to Reg and Loida. "Pam was mugged," I said. "I've got to get back to New York." They both looked concerned. Reg liked Pam, which was a rare thing for him. He thought that she had class. He wanted to know if she was all right. Without hesitation, he told me to head for New York. I was grateful. And that's how I got to spend at least one Thanksgiving at home with my wife. I walked into our apartment and hugged Pam hard. Over a small feast, she recounted her harrowing tale, occasionally tearing up. I realized the cost to Pam of my being away so often, the loneliness we both felt.

Pam had pursued her own path in the city, working as an interior designer. But there was no movement, no upward push. Work for her was more like a hobby than a career. That's the way many spouses felt at the time. One of her friends asked me, "What has she accomplished?" Pam's answer to that question would be, "I'm the CEO of Meily, Inc." She focused on me and my career. But there was one thing she said that stuck in my mind. She vowed that she would never wind up like her mother, having to ask for money from her husband to buy something. I only understood much later how determined she was to be financially independent.

I remembered how once when we were in Manila, Pam took a detour to her family home in the suburbs and surprised me by raising a huge fuss about her sister's impending marriage to a man she didn't like because he constantly borrowed money. There were even rumors that he was already married. Pam dug in her heels in an all-night battle to save her sister from making what to Pam would be the biggest mistake of her life. Pam insisted that her sister could not marry her beau. There was no way that was going to happen. People ran around the house and into the streets screaming and crying. Pam's stubbornness caused a ruckus. The wedding was due to take place in a few days, so I really didn't think that she had a chance of stopping it. But I learned never to underestimate my wife. Pam wouldn't budge until her sister relented and agreed to break off the relationship. The man consented never to see her sister again after getting a small payoff. I watched this drama unfold and realized that the girl that I'd married could be very stubborn and determined when it came to fighting for something dear to her heart. Years later, I would come up against that stubborn streak in a totally different context.

Back in New York, Pam went to enormous trouble to turn our apartment into a home where both of us were comfortable and secure. Pam had installed a folding door in our condo that effectively gave us an extra room. She decorated our place with lamps and plants— actual living things! —and paintings that we purchased from sidewalk vendors or were by unknown artists from her hometown of Zamboanga. She lovingly assembled albums that contained photographs of all the places that we'd visited. A plaque enclosed a small board with a note in white painted on it proclaiming, "You are home" with a tiny heart next to it. A frame filled with colored tiles that spelled out "MEI-LY" greeted guests. Engraved copies of stories about me from my days at the University of Florida and the *Daily News* article about my Dad decorated the walls.

Every now and then, Pam did enjoy certain privileges. Once, Reg flew her over to Paris for the weekend just to deliver documents. Pam visited more often and even negotiated a special discounted rate for me at the Grand Hotel due to my long stays. She drew up plans for where we could visit or dine, lifting me out of my isolation. We'd stop by the small bookstores that lined the Seine, go to Montmartre to shop at a market and then hike up to the Sacre-Coeur Basilica, where we surveyed the city.

We stole away for weekends in London to catch a West End show. Then embarked on a European cruise and sang "Volare" while conga dancing with the passengers. Another time, we drove to Mont St. Michel, that ever-looming castle on a rock in Normandy surrounded by sheep at low tide and sea water at high tide. We took the train over the Alps to Venice where we stayed at the Gritti Hotel. The Gritti was the home of a former nobleman that stood next to the Grand Canal, while nearby was the city's central square, the Piazza San Marco.

Our first morning there, we got up at five. I'd made it a habit to always eat a banana for breakfast no matter where I was. I complained to Pam about not having a banana. All of a sudden, she jumped out of bed and started getting dressed.

"Let's go find a banana."

I looked at her in disbelief.

"C'mon. It'll be fun."

We exited the hotel and began racing around the city. The only ones up were a stray jogger or two. We ran past the canals and crisscrossed the empty streets and bridges. She was so dedicated to pleasing me that she searched everywhere to make sure I had my banana for breakfast. It didn't matter that it was so early in the morning in Venice. It never dawned on us that Venice is an island, and so everything has to be brought in by boat. When we finally located a skiff unloading crates of bananas at the wharf, the crew wouldn't sell us one no matter how much money we offered.

Since we were apart so often, travel was an important part of our relationship. Years later in 1997, we were at the Meurice Hotel in Paris when we heard the screech of cars and motorcycles speeding past our room only to find out the next morning that Princess Diana had died in a car crash. She'd passed us by on her last ride. We rushed to the scene of the accident the next morning and found it crowded with police, news crews, mourners, sightseers and mounds of flowers. Ever the PR man, I asked a TV reporter if he'd be interested in interviewing Pam to get her reaction because she was a Diana fan, but he dismissed me with a wave.

I had met Pam in 1985. I'd met Reg in 1987. Since that time, he'd taken control over my life. For a time, these moments overseas were all we had. I never noticed that my dedication to Reg Lewis might be costing me my marriage.

17 – "LOVING YOU ALWAYS"

After we acquired Beatrice International in 1987, changes were taking place for us not just in Paris but in New York as well. It was as if the Revolution had triumphed and the barbarian horde—that would be us—had breached the inner sanctum of the wealthy and well-pedigreed. The TLC Beatrice cohort in New York City now occupied the palatial offices that once belonged to the executives of RJR Nabisco, captured in a hostile takeover by KKR and broken up. Our offices loomed several floors above KKR itself, the elite takeover firm that had sold us Beatrice International. This fact delighted Reg no end. Gone were the lowly law offices of Lewis & Clarkson. We were now ensconced in magnificent quarters at 9 West 57th Street and Fifth Avenue, overlooking Central Park, just a stone's throw from where I had used to work for Curtis Hoxter years before but a world away. My office was spacious, with a big wooden desk, a TV and steel file cabinets behind me. On my right was a huge picture window from which I could see the people in the Park, tiny figures darting below. Much of midtown Manhattan along with the entirety of the Park's 834 acres lay spread out before me, bordered by Fifth Avenue on the right and Central Park West on the left. As Loida observed, "You get four shows a year," because the Park and its colors changed with every season.

Reg and Loida had always had a home in the Hamptons. But after the Beatrice deal, he decided to trade up. Reg bought Broadview, a grand old mansion set on five and half acres that stood 75 feet above Gardiner's Bay in the town of Amagansett, East Hampton, Long Island. Some 560 feet of white, sandy beach lay below it. The property cost $3.6 million. Amagansett was one of the enclaves for the well-to-do and famous. The imposing, gray-paneled house was part of what used to be known as the Bell Estate. It was a 21-room Georgian-style home that featured air-conditioning, a heated pool, and an all-weather tennis court. A well-manicured lawn stretched from the entrance and along the winding driveway to the parking area below the house. On the other side lay the water, extending as far as you could see. The Hamptons formed part of New York City's summer social scene where the rich and the wanna-be rich mingled and partied. Reg jumped from a wanna-be to a genuine member of the fraternity, at least as far as a Black person could hope to be back then. He even received a note from Mrs. Brooke Astor, one of New York City's true aristocrats, inviting him to a social function. That was a signal that he'd arrived.

Mayor David Dinkins of New York City visited regularly and played tennis with Reg, who, as in everything else he did, played the sport intensely and well. Another regular visitor was Arthur Ashe, the celebrated African-American tennis player who'd won the U.S. Open in 1968. So were opera stars and Wall Street types. Reg loved it. It relaxed him to be there, lounging on a lawn chair in his tennis whites while puffing on a cigar. It fit his image of who he now was.

Loida hosted a birthday party for him once in Broadview with an orchestra playing tunes from Cole Porter and George Gershwin. Everyone was decked out in fashionable Hamptons summer outfits. The romantic notes of "Moonlight Serenade" wafted over the house, and I took Pam in my arms and danced, a rarity.

Just then we heard a plane thunder overhead. It began to paint something across the sky in big bold letters. We shaded our eyes against the sun so we could make out the writing. It said: **"Reg, Loving You Always, Loida."** Everybody applauded and drank a toast.

"There she goes again," Reg said to gales of drunken laughter. "Spending my money." Then Reg whispered to Loida, "Did you ever think we would come this far?"

"I always knew you could do it, darling."

"You've got to admit, this is pretty good," he grinned. Then he suddenly looked anxious. "Sometimes it's hard for me to believe it myself. I wake up at night worrying somebody's going to take it all away from me."

"Nobody's going to do that, Reg. What you have, you've earned."

Now and then, we held more intimate parties, with no more than a few carefully chosen guests, usually young, pretty girls out for a good time. What Reg did, he did. Any affairs he chose to indulge in weren't my business. I didn't believe that it was part of my mandate to sit in judgment on the private life of anybody. Or maybe that was just a convenient excuse for acting as an accomplice. I liked Loida. After all, she had made the call that got me the job. But Reg succeeded in winning me over to his side. He trusted me completely, confiding in me both his professional and personal plans.

Once, Jean Pierre told me that Reg had a habit of grading everyone who worked for him from A to F. He'd put all the names down on a sheet of yellow legal-size paper. He often talked to Jean Pierre as he graded, commenting about each of us as he penciled in a mark.

"Butch, you were the only one who received an A," Jean Pierre told me in that soft French accent of his.

"You're joking?" I felt proud. Reg appreciated my loyalty, hard work, and sacrifice after all.

"I'm not joking," Jean Pierre said. "Out of everyone in the office, you were the only one who had an A next to his name."

I grinned. I decided not to ask him what grade he'd gotten.

There was a time when it was just Reg and me who flew off to stay at Hotel du Cap-Eden-Roc in Antibes in the south of France. Built in 1870, the hotel stood on a bluff overlooking the Mediterranean, the playground of the rich and famous from the days of the writer F. Scott Fitzgerald and to this day, a hangout for movie stars during the annual Cannes film festival. The main building looked like a castle; its restaurant gazed out at rocks below and the ocean beyond; the staff were both helpful and arrogant. Reg certainly knew the right places to stay and seemed to know the secret code that let you in to a different world from the one the rest of us inhabited. We worked during the daytime in between two rounds of tennis.

I functioned as Reg's link to the boys back in New York. We called them daily on a speaker phone and questioned them closely, although I suspected they headed out to long lunches right after they spoke to us. I acted as his cover, too; because at night, he snuck away in a car with this beautiful Senegalese woman who was always pleasant to me. She often wore these long, flowing gowns in pink or black. I called her Madame. They drove off to the casino at Monte Carlo while I was left on my own, which was fine with me. I needed time off from Reg. Again, I decided it was his business. I did not judge him to be better or worse than anyone else. I couldn't bring myself to turn on him although I did feel bad for Loida. She loved him no matter what. From comments that she'd make occasionally — "That's the way men are" and "Women have to learn to overlook these things"—I could tell that she came from a different generation, one that believed that women had to put up with it all. "I knew he loved me and that at the end of the day, he would come home to me," Loida later said.

Reg regularly screamed at her, even humiliated her in front of guests and the household staff. Once, after news came that Avon, the cosmetics company, had bought Tiffany, she told him in front of some visitors that she was surprised by the acquisition because she'd always thought that Tiffany was the larger company. Reg yelled that she was stupid for thinking that because Avon Products was so much bigger. Few other wives would have put up with it but she, like the rest of us, just stood there and took it. Her love remained undiminished.

"Darling, if you want to walk out of this marriage," she once told him, "go ahead. But I will never leave you."

I often wondered why she ignored all the goings on, but it must have been her faith, her deep-seated belief in a God that looked out for her and for all the rest of us. In later years, that belief in a deity that lay outside of anything we could see or touch would bolster her, and I guess myself, during many hard times to come.

18 – KEEP GOING, NO MATTER WHAT

We now possessed more than a dozen European food companies with head-quarters in both New York and Paris. But Reg convinced himself that we needed the ultimate big-boy toy. He decided to buy his own plane, a new one. He went about it with his customary thoroughness. He studied all the different models, leafed carefully through the manuals, and talked extensively to aviation experts.

Finally, he settled on purchasing a Challenger jet and we wound up visiting the Bombardier factory in Montreal where the Challengers were man-ufactured. It was a giant facility with dozens of machines housed in ware-house-type buildings that churned out airplane parts, while in one huge hangar stood spiffy Challenger jets equipped with the latest technology.

Reg wanted his plane straight off the factory floor, built to his specifica-tions. He chose the colors, the carpet, the bathroom fixtures. It was to be a big, roomy cabin with light brown panels so that it gave off a bright, cheery feel-ing during those long hours of flight. He even commissioned a well-known African American artist, Ed Clark, to paint an original modernist mural that covered the entire front cabin door and wall of the aircraft so the passengers could see it throughout the flight. From time to time, we visited the plane to see how Ed was coming along on his masterpiece. The Challenger was like Reg's home away from home and he liked his art.

The transatlantic flights from New York to Paris were the highlight. Reg picked the movies and the menu, even the music (typically Anita Baker and Whitney Houston). Everything was first class, and I have to say, nothing beats flying in your own plane.

"Let's put on *American in Paris*," Reg announced to us once.

"Reg, we just watched that movie the last time we flew over," I moaned.

"Who cares? Whose airplane is this, anyway?" he blurted out, and we all settled in to watch Gene Kelly dance through the streets of Paris. Reg, too, was very much an American in Paris, and proud of it. He saw himself as the star in his own movie. He relished watching the film. Sometimes he'd sing along with Gene Kelly.

"We may be in decline," he told us about America in an aside, "but we're good for another 100 to 200 years."

One evening, while Reg was sleeping and Anita Baker was crooning in the background, the captain, Brendan Flannery, a former helicopter pilot in Vietnam, asked me to come up to the cockpit so I could see the aurora borealis. I watched this spectral display of colored lights that swirled before us in the night sky with awe. I felt lucky to be alive and, in that moment, I wanted to grab hold of those lights and travel the universe.

We took that plane everywhere. We flew off early in the morning from Le Bourget, where Lindbergh had landed his single-engine aircraft after piloting the first trans-Atlantic flight all those decades ago. We'd hit three or four European cities a day, Milan, Amsterdam, Madrid, Dublin, before finally returning home, tired. I got used to seeing that miniature Statue of Liberty on the Seine River as we drove by it early in the morning and then again lit up late at night as we drove home.

Reg was content to let the European managers run the operations, but he wanted to be an active owner. He wanted to see and be seen. And I was there right by his side, an "eminence grise" or grey eminence, his sounding board, someone he could talk to about anything in a way he couldn't even with his wife. What did you think of so and so? Do you think he was insulting me? What did you take out of the meeting? He'd pepper me with questions before venting about a professional or personal problem.

I wrote the company's earnings releases and Reg's speeches, at least to the point of getting him a first draft that he would then rewrite and fiddle with endlessly. He demanded that I call reporters to complain about how they covered Beatrice International's earnings which turned much of the media off. Jonathan Hicks of the *New York Times*, one of our closest friends, wrote a short piece about our quarterly earnings once and placed it prominently in a box on the front page of the business section. But because there were one or two words in the story that indicated a downward trend in our profits, it set Reg off. He didn't understand that we did not write the stories. Reporters did and they were independent observers and not on our payroll. So, in truth, even a story that was 80 percent favorable was a victory.

Nevertheless, I dutifully called Hicks to complain, and he was understandably upset. "Couldn't you call him and just talk about baseball, just so you could tell Reg you called?" said Chris Atkins, my former boss at Burson, when I told him about it.

Once, when we flew to Verona to negotiate with old man Sanson at the headquarters of his ice cream company, Reg visited a shoe factory and ordered several pairs of custom-made Italian shoes. I viewed the famous balcony from where, supposedly, Shakespeare's lovers Romeo and Juliet acted out their ill-fated romance. I later had to fly back to Verona on the jet with one of our European staff, an odd fellow, Andrea Nutti, who with his loose hair sprouting in all directions, glasses and Italian accent resembled an absent-minded professor. Our mission, with Nutti acting as translator and aide, was to pick up Reg's precious custom-made pairs of shoes and fly them to Paris.

One day, Reg and Loida flew off to St. Moritz to meet some jetsetter friends for a party. The guests were part of a very European collection of faded aristocrats and wealthy people from Iran and the Middle East. They skied while I stayed behind at the Palace Hotel, the first version of which was built in 1896. Good thing they'd updated the plumbing. The hotel lay in a valley surrounded by snow-covered mountains on one side and a lake on the other. It had a lobby that seemed to stretch out forever. I took the gondola up the mountain on my own, just to take in the view. I squeezed in with these kids in ski suits who were all talking in Romansh, a dialect left over from the days of the Romans based on Latin and spoken only in the Swiss Alps.

Then I determined to go tramping around that frozen lake all by myself. I had to get away from Reg no matter what. Nobody else was fool enough to do it in the dead of winter. It was so cold that I couldn't stop shivering underneath my heavy coat and long underwear. But those chilly walks kept me sane. Because being with the boss 100 percent of the time—as I nearly was - wasn't my idea of a happy life. Sometimes I just needed to break away on my own and I didn't care what the weather was. I simply sat by the lake trembling but content, luxuriating in my solitude. By this time, I was making from $150,000 to $300,000 a year, depending on our bonus, but I began to wonder if the money was worth it. I had risen to the heights of American business in a short time, and, for a Filipino immigrant, it felt pretty heady. But I sensed I was losing something of myself in the process, self-respect, confidence, a life outside of work of any kind. And looking back, the love that I had anchored my life on was melting away as well.

Some of it was my fault. Such as that one night with a baroness during our stay in St. Moritz. I was a man after all and if there was an open door, I was going to walk through it. She was older and perhaps a little overweight, but I didn't mind. "She's in room 421," her friend whispered to me. I tiptoed up the stairs and slowly opened the door and found it to be conveniently unlocked. The baroness had sat beside me at dinner all night and I rushed to her bed. She pretended to be asleep, and I woke her with a kiss. She smiled at me, not at all surprised. Then she closed her eyes and I undressed her with alacrity ….

The next morning, Reg complained that he'd rung my room all night and there was no answer while Loida herself had gone looking for me in the lobby. Shit! That was unlucky. Putting on my best poker face, I proclaimed that I was in my room all evening, fast asleep and hadn't heard a thing. They stared at me, annoyed and skeptical.

Often, since I spent a lot of time waiting for Reg, it was the drivers who'd become my best friends. I treated everyone the same and met interesting personalities. Patrick, our driver in Paris, asked Reg every evening when he dropped him off at home, "Monsieur Lewis, what time should I show up tomorrow morning?" Reg would pretend to think about it, then declare, "7 a.m.," even though he seldom left the apartment till 9 or 9:30. It was like a routine we went through, with Patrick always asking the same question and hoping that he'd get a different answer; Reg furrowing his brow, pondering, and then giving the same answer every time. I could almost see him grinning to himself.

In St. Moritz, I became friends with our chauffeur, an older, balding Swiss fellow. While we were waiting around once, he invited me to his favorite coffee shop. The owner and he shared a big laugh when I ordered a hot chocolate.

"Only little children drink that," he said as they guffawed. When we finally left St. Moritz, he seemed sad and told me that I could use his condo anytime I wanted to visit. We were like veterans who'd been to war together.

"That's the way it is in this business. You become friends with someone and then one day, they fly off and you'll never see them again," he shrugged philosophically. I shook his hand warmly and promised I'd be back. But I never saw him or St. Moritz again.

When we were in Paris, we watched CNN in order to catch up on the news in the U.S. One time, Reg and I were watching President Clinton's inauguration and I could sense Reg's angst. Clinton and he were from the same generation and Reg was always competitive. We explored the idea of him running for the U.S. Senate, perhaps for the seat in Maryland, his home state. After all, we had the resources and the plane to get us from one stop to another quickly.

"Run to the right on defense and foreign policy and to the left on social policy. Like Scoop Jackson (a senator who had unsuccessfully run for president). That's the plan," he'd say as we discussed his options.

"Once I get into the Senate, anything could happen. Lightning could strike!" He laughed loudly. He intimated to Jean Pierre that maybe he could become President of the United States someday. "We're going to be in the White House, Jean Pierre." Nothing seemed beyond his reach. But we never got beyond talking about the idea. You have to have a thick skin to go into politics and Reg did not possess that.

Another time, we watched as real estate developer Donald Trump hawked his latest project.

"I can't believe this guy," I grumbled. "He's got a hell of an ego. He's using his name as a brand to sell his buildings."

Reg gave me a look. "What are you getting on his case for? The guy's just trying to earn a living." Reg's attitude brought me up short. I guess he admired Trump because he was hustling and using his marketing savvy to make money.

Back in New York, Reg became the city's darling. Anytime people knew that I worked for him or anytime I mentioned his name, their ears would perk up. They knew who he was. He was also a folk hero to the African American community nationwide. We received letters from people around the country, particularly after an article ran about him. "The guy that bought Beatrice," they called him knowingly.

Reg was generous to Black causes. Every Christmas Eve, I personally took a car and delivered checks from him to different groups. Reverend Calvin Butts of the Abyssinian Baptist Church in Harlem was a particular favorite. I alighted from the car and tried to tiptoe my way into the church unnoticed. Every time he spotted me though, he would shout out to the congregation in glee, "My brothers, hark! One of the three Wise Men has arrived."

The annual Columbia University Paul Robeson gala was one of the high points for the community in New York. It brought out the upper class among the city's African American population. One year, Reg was chosen as the honoree, appropriate because Robeson and Reg had both become icons for the

Black community. Not only was Robeson a great artist, he'd pursued a path of political activism that influenced many. In Reg's case, his contributions to charities and his breaking of color barriers throughout his life made him a role model for people. In the 1970's, Reg flew to North Carolina to defend the Reverend Ben Chavis, a campaigner for civil rights who was unjustly charged for conspiracy and arson as part of what was known as the Wilmington Ten. It became an internationally celebrated case and Reg's courageous decision to act as Chavis' attorney demonstrated that he was more than just a hard-nosed businessman.

Reg asked me to write a draft of his talk accepting the Paul Robeson award. From my years in the PR business, I'd learned that to come up with a good speech, it's best to interview your client so that you can find out what he wants to say and get a feel for his language and cadence. You want to use as many of his own words as you can so the finished product comes as close as possible to something he would say. I carefully labored on the draft and turned it in. He studied it closely, then said, to my surprise, "I like it," and began marking it up with his black pen.

I could see the speech was important to him. He called the TLC boys in so we could watch him practice his lines, another good idea. He told me to add a Langston Hughes poem, "Mother to Son," that he particularly liked. The words captured his sense of struggling against the odds and the reality that his path had not been easy.

Reg read the poem aloud. "'So, boy, don't you turn back . . . Don't you fall now—For I'se still goin', honey. I'se still climbin', And life for me ain't been no crystal stair.'"

I could tell that those lines from the poem meant a lot to Reg just from the way he read them to me. Then he turned to me to explain. "Butch, life for me ain't been no crystal stair. I told you before. I'm no overnight success, no matter what the press says. It took me years of hard work to make it. That's what people don't understand."

It was true. Success is always the product of years of preparation and labor. In Reg's case, he had first worked as a lawyer at Paul Weiss and then struck out on his own and started his own law firm. He labored mostly on government-mandated minority venture capital deals, known as MESBICs, where he became notorious for insisting on getting paid by his clients without delay. He moved on to do his own deals through TLC Group, attempting leveraged buyouts that never came to pass until he finally succeeded in acquiring Mc-Call Pattern in 1984 and then the big one, Beatrice International, in 1987.

As we talked some more, Reg spoke about how important it was to keep going, no matter what. He'd said it almost casually but his remark struck a chord with me. I wrote it on my ever-present yellow legal pad.

Reg took everything seriously, but at the top of the list was any kind of public appearance, particularly a speech. He was very concerned with how he appeared to people. Reg was both tense and intense before a speech, and that was especially stressful to everyone at the office. The night of the Robeson dinner, I dropped by his home because we normally rode together to these affairs. Loida, stylishly attired as usual in a black Parisian gown, joined us.

Reg was in black tie and even more nervous than usual, an anxiety manifested in bouts of screaming. It was aimed at any convenient target: Loida, the maid, John the driver or, for that matter, me. We tumbled into the Bentley feeling enormously stressed and all through the ride from Reg's apartment in downtown Chelsea to Columbia University on the Upper West Side, he took off on a wild rant.

"What the fuck, Loida? Why are you wearing that? Don't you have any taste? . . . What are you looking at, Butch? This is a lousy speech! And I'm the one who has to get up there and deliver it. Not you or anyone else . . . . Baffoe, what the fuck are you doing? Why are you taking Eighth Avenue instead of the West Side Highway? I'm going to fire your ass! You too, Butch! Loida, you picked out the wrong cuff links! You're no help at all. You're all a bunch of clowns!"

He was trembling with rage so much so that the car itself seemed to be shaking from all the screaming. John could hardly keep his hands steady on the wheel. I wanted to jump out of the window even if it killed me. John and I were embarrassed at how Reg was treating Loida. We could not wait till we arrived at Columbia. Loida simply sat through the whole tantrum, stoic and silent. I think she realized that anything she said would just add fuel to the fire.

Finally, the car pulled up to the school and out stepped Reg in his tux, and it was like a light clicked on. All of a sudden, he turned on the charm. He was all smiles, moving easily through the crowd, shaking hands, whispering witticisms. I could hardly believe my eyes as I watched him greet everyone and make small talk while Loida and I could barely stand up straight after the shellacking we'd taken. We avoided looking at each other but I sensed her pain.

To top it all, Reg then proceeded to deliver one of the greatest speeches of his life. I can still hear his words:

"So, in the quiet of that room, I would think about the great men and women that have gone before me and the enormous obstacles that they had to overcome. And the moment I'd begin to whine and just feel down, I'd think that my parents, my grandparents and their parents were with me . . . and all of a sudden there rose this enormous chorus that was saying, . . . keep going, no matter what. So, for me ladies and gentlemen, I think if Paul Robeson were here tonight, the one message he'd give and that I share is, 'Keep going, no matter what.'"

I'd taken that phrase, "Keep going, no matter what," from our talks and used it as the ending for his speech. "Keep going, no matter what" later became something of an anthem for him that we would come back to again and again in his speeches.

The audience went wild. And I can tell you the car ride back home was 180 degrees different from the ride over. He laughed and asked us how he'd done and told us what so-and-so said to him. At home, we drank champagne to celebrate. He was overjoyed.

But deep down inside me, I was unable to forget the tirade he'd sprayed around the car at us for 40 minutes. And I said to myself, "I can't take this forever."

Sooner or later, something had to give.

Joe Meily Jr. poses with his family during Christmas in the early 1960s at their home in Loyola Heights, Metro Manila. From left to right, Rose (standing), Tess, Jim, Anita Meily, Finina, Joe, Susan and Butch (standing).

Butch Meily poses with his proud father, Joe Meily Jr., in his TLC Beatrice International office overlooking New York City and Central Park in Manhattan's 9 West 57th Street building.

Butch and Pam Meily at her uncle's Sutton Place apartment in Manhattan soon after their first meeting in 1987.

Butch Meily stands on the steps of a Federal building in Manhattan in 1991 on the day he received his American citizenship due to this father's wartime service.

Trans-Atlantic trip between New York and Paris on the TLC Beatrice International Challenger jet with (from left to right): David Guarino, Controller, Mark Thorne, Chief Financial Officer, Butch Meily, Public Relations, Carl Brody, Tax, and Everett Grant, Finance. Reginald Lewis later commissioned African American artist Ed Clark to paint a mural on the cabin wall behind them.

Butch Meily, Reginald Lewis, and Jean Pierre Tegnet preparing for a party at Lewis' Place du Palais Bourbon residence in Paris.

Reginald Lewis walking off the TLC Beatrice plane with executives. Butch Meily is seen bringing up the left rear. Courtesy of RFL Photos.

Butch and Marco Meily at their Woodstock, New York country home.

Butch, Marco, and Pam Meily in New York City.

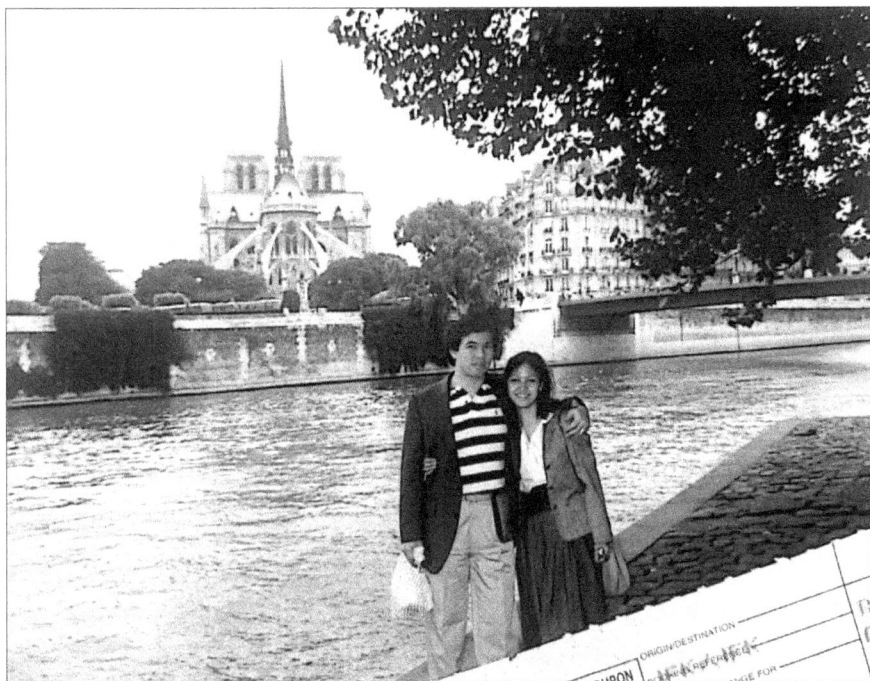

Butch and Pam Meily in Paris with the Notre Dame cathedral in the background.

Butch Meily and Jean Pierre Tegnet at a party in Place du Palais Bourbon residence in Paris of Reginald and Loida Lewis.

Pam and Butch Meily with New York City Mayor David Dinkins at Loida Lewis' home in the Hamptons, New York.

Butch and Pam Meily pose with Reginald Lewis' Amagansett, Long Island home in the background. The mansion burned down in 1991.

Reginald Lewis relaxing at his Broadview mansion in Amagansett, Long Island with Jean Pierre Tegnet and Delma, the cook. The house later burned down.

TLC Group relaxing at Reginald Lewis' Broadview mansion in Amagansett, the Hamptons, Long Island. Everett Grant, Mrs. Kevin Wright, Butch and Pam Meily, Reginald and Loida Lewis, Kevin Wright and son, Mrs. Everett Grant, David Guarino and Jean Pierre Tegnet.

Joe Meily Jr. taking batting practice in the New York Yankees dugout on the day a New York Daily News columnist took him and his son Butch to a game.

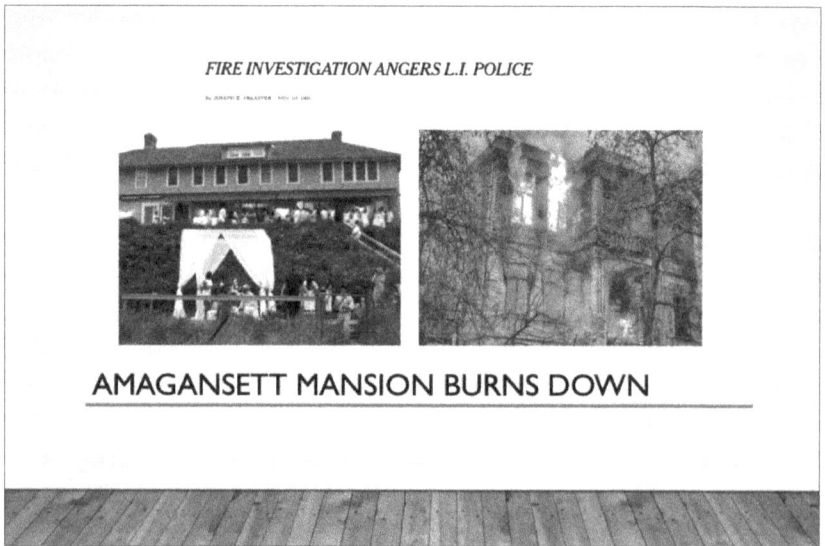

FIRE INVESTIGATION ANGERS L.I. POLICE

AMAGANSETT MANSION BURNS DOWN

Reginald Lewis's Amagansett mansion before and after it burned down in 1991.

19 – "WE COULD HAVE MADE HISTORY, BUTCH"

Diana Ross started singing one of her signature songs, "Touch Me in the Morning," to an audience that included some of the preeminent takeover pirates in the country. The occasion was Drexel Burnham Lambert's annual High Yield Bond Conference at the Beverly Hills Hilton Hotel. As she crooned, she gazed out at the crowd till she finally picked out the lucky person on whose lap she would sit while she sang. It was Reginald Lewis.

There was one event that stood out from all the rest in our schedule and that was Drexel's gathering, informally known in the industry as the Predators' Ball. The Beverly Hills Hilton featured palm trees, tropical plants, and a large ballroom. No expense was spared, and we were treated to the finest food and entertainment. People stayed up all night drinking at the Polo Lounge and then headed straight into the conference. Mike Milken was the host and the people who attended included such luminaries as Ron Perelman, Carl Icahn, Sir James Goldsmith, the British raider. Back then, Leon Black who years later established one of the largest hedge funds in the world, scurried around carrying out Mike's orders. Robber barons, scalawags, and rebels were there, all now captains of industry. It was like a business version of a Mafia reunion.

There were talks, intellectual discussions and presentations, and numerous showings of Drexel ads about how junk bonds were building the country to the tune of Jefferson Starship's "We Built This City." But the real business took place outside the conference halls and focused on which company was in play, who was going to be the next takeover target. After the Beatrice International deal in 1987, Reg became part of the team, the only Black member as far as I could tell.

At several desks outside, the staff gave away mugs and bags with the Drexel name on them. Even though everyone here was earning good money, they were aggressive when it came to the freebies. One man in an expensive suit pushed another guy out of the way to grab a Drexel bag.

"Watch it, buddy."

"Fuck you. I'm getting mine."

"Fuck you too. I want that bag!"

"People, please. We'll get you more of the bags in a few minutes."

For me, it all felt exhilarating. It became a fact of life, like waking up in the morning. None of us ever thought it would end.

By 1989, we continued to do well. We were flying high. After selling off operations to pay down debt, Reg and his team had pared TLC Beatrice International down to a European core of food companies that were market leaders. He'd increased revenues. For the previous year, the company earned $50 million on sales of $1.02 billion. He'd reduced debt to just $100 million with all the asset sales.

Reg's image was good. It was time to soar to yet another level. Merrill Lynch courted him and asked him to take TLC Beatrice public. The head of the New York Stock Exchange met with him and begged him to grab the opportunity to have his company become the first Black-controlled entity listed on the Exchange with him as its CEO and principal owner. After much thought, Reg decided to launch a public offering of stock of TLC Beatrice International. That was going to be historical, yet another door Reg would kick in to force his way into the establishment. Besides, the Drexel guys were impatient to cash in on their TLC Beatrice stock. An initial public offering, or IPO, would allow them to sell their shares at a hefty premium. I was excited. This was going to be another step up for all of us and although I was tired, I looked forward to getting the deal done.

Reg and I plotted the announcement carefully. We'd start just like we did with the initial disclosure of the Beatrice acquisition in 1987. Jonathan Hicks from *The Times* promised us the front page of the business section above the fold with a photo in exchange for an exclusive. It happened just as we'd planned, almost. In November 1989, Hicks' *New York Times* article fired the opening gun of our campaign with the headline, "TLC Offers 35% Stake to the Public."

TLC Beatrice International Inc., the international food company controlled by the Wall Street investor Reginald F. Lewis, said yesterday that the company would sell a 35 percent stake to the public to raise as much as $194 million. The company said the offering of 18.5 million shares, at prices of $9 to $10.50 a share, would *enable it to retire the remaining high yield debt incurred from the acquisition of Beatrice International. The offering would leave Mr. Lewis, the chairman and chief executive of the company, with 58 percent of the shares. It would also make TLC the first black-owned company to be listed on the New York Stock Exchange…Some analysts said the proceeds from the offering might be used for acquisitions by Mr. Lewis, possibly in the food products industry in the United States (our sources)…. Mr. Lewis said in a phone interview (that was me and Jonathan with him) that, 'You do something like this because you want to have as wide an array of capital sources as possible to grow…A successful company in today's world has to have broad exposure to the capital markets.'*

"You mustn't forget the F, Butch," Reg kept telling me about his middle initial, though there were plenty of jokes among the guys in New York about what the F really stood for. Yes, it was all there. We would use the money to pay down our debt and potentially buy other companies, this time in the U.S. Reg had been eying the domestic operations of Beatrice for some time. It had all the name brands—Tropicana Orange Juice, Samsonite luggage, Orville Redenbacher Popcorn. We were looking at other targets too. I recall that once, the entire TLC Beatrice team, including a bevy of lawyers and accountants, crowded onto our plane to fly to Detroit to try to buy Chrysler from its CEO Lee Iacocca. Anything seemed possible for Reg. He wanted to be big in America as well, not just in Paris.

We were supremely confident. We had a good story to tell. And, at least as long as I'd been with him, Reg had never failed at anything. We took our plane and set out on a global roadshow. This was what they call those meetings with potential investors where you get to tell your story and answer questions. It was like opening a show on Broadway. We toured Zurich, London, and Paris; after all, these were European assets. The response was promising. People appeared enthusiastic.

Surely, nothing could prevent us from yet another spectacular success.

When we got to Paris though, I got a troubling phone call. It was *Barron's*, a heavyweight financial publication in New York. They planned to do a story on the offering. At first, I naïvely expected the story would be like all the others, praising the bold African American entrepreneur. But the more I learned about the reporter's angle, the more concerned I got. The tenor of his questions appeared to paint the public offering as nothing more than an exercise in greed. Mike Milken and his gang were using the IPO to cash out at an enormous multiple to their original investment. Reg's compensation resulting from the deal was also an issue. He would earn $16 million, equivalent to $39.4 million today. $16 million a year back then was a lot of money, even for a CEO. In addition, *Barron's* questioned the veracity of Beatrice's cash flow, which was all in foreign currencies. Because we were earning in Italian liras, French francs, Spanish pesetas, Irish pounds, they raised doubts about what the true value was in U.S. dollars and how reliable these earnings would be in the future due to fluctuations in the currency exchange rate.

This sounded threatening. It could upend the whole enterprise, I realized. I discussed it with Reg. He was in the middle of one of his parties at the residence on Palais Bourbon, but he recognized the danger and he immediately dispatched Everett Grant, our financial guy from TLC, to join me and talk to the *Barron's* reporter on the phone.

"Get him off that angle," Reg ordered.

We left the party and found a quiet room in the house where we wound up speaking to the writer for hours. "But Reed, you have to consider that the company's earnings are excellent. The Beatrice companies are all market leaders in these countries." Everett and I struggled to explain our side. But nothing we said swayed him from his story. He just kept repeating his version of the transaction. His agenda was set from the start. This was not an interview. He was talking to us merely so he could say he'd spoken to us and gotten our views.

I started losing sleep. I popped a sleeping pill a night. I dreaded what the story would say and what it's effect would be on the public offering. *Barron's* carried a great deal of weight in the financial community. Their negative story with its accusations about the IPO being a tool for the Drexel group and Reg to rake in a pile of money would set the tone for coverage of our public offering and color the perceptions of investors globally. It could torpedo the IPO and tarnish Reg and the company's image for years to come. Now I understood what people meant when they said working with the press could be a double-edged sword. I wasn't used to negative stories. We'd had it so good for so long. But Everett waved it off. What are you going to do? he seemed to suggest. Even Reg lapsed into an uncharacteristic complacency. They didn't seem to appreciate how a negative story in *Barron's* could impact our public offering. I hoped against hope that the article would come out all right, that we would survive any ill effects.

By the time we landed in Baltimore, Reg's hometown, to host more investor briefings, the *Barron's* story had hit the streets. It was a very extensive, detailed article, all of it negative. Wall Street took notice. The first sign of trouble was that fewer people showed up at our roadshow meetings. We got worried phone calls from our investment bankers. Investors began to cool on the Beatrice stock offering that I had trumpeted with such promise. Our historic IPO was beginning to look iffy. We were like a play that had gotten a bad review in previews. I knew we were in a hole, and I wasn't sure if we could climb out of it. We wrote a letter to the editor of *Barron's*, disputing in great detail every point in the article. They printed our letter alongside their rebuttal of our letter. They were going for the kill.

Merrill Lynch, the firm managing the IPO, hurried to our offices. They were anxious. We crammed into Reg's office with all of us jammed next to each other on the sofa while others sat on armrests or chairs that they hauled in. The bankers were apologetic that the offering wasn't going as planned. The TLC team was worried that the IPO might be sinking fast. Merrill asked Reg if he would be willing to reduce the share price and cut his compensation. They felt that if the Beatrice stock were priced lower, the offering could still succeed. A lower salary for the CEO would defuse that issue. The problem was that decreasing the share price meant lowering the value of the company.

"No fucking way," Reg said. He was adamant: He wanted to get paid like everyone else. He kept repeating that Milken received $550 million for one year's work. Next to that, his compensation was nothing.

He'd rather see the IPO go down than lower the value of the company or reduce his salary, he said. None of us contradicted him. We sleepwalked through the whole exercise. No one volunteered any ideas on how to save our IPO. Within days, the offering was dead. I distributed a one-paragraph press release saying that we'd withdrawn the offering. I heard that the editors at *Barron's* celebrated when they learned that we'd pulled the offering and put the story of our retreat up on a bulletin board, like a trophy on a fireplace mantle.

It was Reg's first public defeat, and the media coverage reflected it. "Business History Deferred, The TLC Beatrice IPO," mourned *Black Enterprise*. He was no longer a superhero who could do no wrong. The dream of a Black-led company being listed on the New York Stock Exchange faded away.

"We could have made history, Butch," Reg told me once wistfully. "The first company listed on the New York Stock Exchange to be owned and controlled by a Black man. That would have been something. And you'd have been part of it."

"We came pretty close, Reg," I replied. I felt responsible. After all, media relations was my specialty. Could I have handled *Barron's* differently, I kept asking myself. Maybe we shouldn't have announced the IPO with such a flourish in the papers and just kept our public offering under the radar. I'd had a long string of successes going all the way back to my Chicago days but sometimes your luck runs out.

Years later, Harold Burson, the founder of Burson Marsteller and consiglieri to many Fortune 500 CEOs, spoke to Reg about the IPO. He asked him if he would have taken a salary cut if it had meant being able to get the transaction done. Reg shook his head, no. As I walked Harold out of Reg's office, he whispered to me, "There was nothing you could have done."

Reg seemed to sense our collective disappointment and we were surprised to get larger than usual bonuses that Christmas. Reg's practice was to call each of us into his office one by one the week before Christmas and that's when he'd tell us what we were getting. Our wives, several of whom were not working, were especially eager to know the figures. I myself received $150,000 which took a little bit of the sting out of the IPO defeat.

20 – "GET IN THE BACK OF THE CAR"

Reg was different after the Initial Public Offering failed. The debacle took something out of him. The intensity, the rage was still there but some of his confidence, his bravado, the sense of inevitability that he'd worn ever since the sale of McCall Pattern was gone. The recurring tension in the office grew worse. He lost his temper more frequently. His incessant yelling which had increased wore me down. I was one of his favorite targets.

"That's what I like about you," he told me one day. "All the screaming doesn't seem to bother you."

This had a certain truth to it. I did a pretty good job of being his lightning rod, absorbing his anger. After all, I'd had a lot of practice going back to that first car ride from *The New York Times*. But he was mistaken. All the browbeating bothered me. It bothered me plenty. It took a toll on me, sapping my confidence. You get yelled at often enough and it diminishes your self-respect, as Cleve from TLC Group reminded me once. You doubt yourself more.

Someone has to be very close to you to be comfortable enough to show you who they really are. And that's how I interpreted Reg's tantrums directed at me. He was under tremendous pressure. Pressure to keep Beatrice's profits pointing upward. Pressure to excel at everything he tried. Pressure that came mostly from himself. His family and a few of us at the office were the only ones who were close to him and he shared secrets with me that he didn't with anyone else. What a privilege, I grimaced. I could always leave the job, of course, but he was paying me too much to even consider it. Yet leaving was exactly what I was thinking about more and more.

Reg wanted everything you had to give, all of your time and your attention. He paid us well. But there were those at TLC who still complained. "He promised he'd make us all rich but that never happened," moaned one of the guys.

Most seriously, the job took me away from Pam or any semblance of a family or a life at home. Just taking a few days off was not easy. During one Fourth of July weekend, he called Lessa, my sister-in-law, continuously to find out where I was. "What do you mean you don't know where Butch is? Aren't you his sister-in-law?" In Paris, we were almost completely his.

We didn't even have the time to start a family. I was never home long enough or even relaxed enough to consider it. Pam pressured me to have kids.

"Butch, if we don't start soon, I may not be able to have children," she finally told me straight.

I told myself maybe it was time to get off the bus.

One day when we were alone at the Beatrice office in New York, he and I had a talk in earnest. I began by telling Reg that I needed to spend more time with Pam. He demurred.

"I thought that was part of the deal," Reg said. "That if I paid you enough, you'd give up time with your family."

I shook my head. "That's not how it works. Not for me."

"Nothing in life comes for free, Butch. There's a price we pay for the life we choose to lead."

Reg's eyes clawed into me. I kept quiet. I told myself, you've got to be sure before you cross this bridge. I backed away from giving him an ultimatum about my staying with the company.

"I don't think I can handle much more of this," I told Pam that evening. "Every day is like a fistfight. I go to work each morning with a knot in my stomach, wondering what it is that I'm going to get yelled at. Sunday evenings are the worst. I get depressed when I start thinking about going into the office the next day."

"Where will you go? What else can you do? It might be hard to earn as much money someplace else," she said bluntly, her arms folded as she faced me.

"I don't know," I said, "but I may not last much longer. I'd be willing to take less money. There's always the PR agencies."

Neither of us felt enthusiastic about that possibility. But I was ready to live a scaled down lifestyle if that meant more time at home and the chance to have children.

About a month later, the issue came to a boil. During one of our meetings at the Beatrice offices in New York, Reg stopped himself in mid-sentence and looked at the guys.

"Hey fellows," he said, "I was just wondering. Would you be willing to take a bullet for me?"

Unsettled by the query, we were silent. What was the correct answer? I wondered.

"It seems like a fair question," Reg said. "After all, I pay you all a hell of a lot of money."

We glanced uneasily at one another. Then we heard a voice.

"I'd take a bullet for you, Reg," said David Guarino, our pimply-faced controller, with a whimper.

We glared at him. He tended to parrot whatever he thought Reg wanted to hear.

"That's what I thought," Reg said with disgust. Was he disgusted at David? Or with the rest of us for our silence? I was unsure. It sounded like a strange question, but for Reg, or at least for the Reg he was becoming, it seemed perfectly normal. He had always been demanding, but now he was worse. Everything seemed to revolve around his ego. The others blamed me.

"This is all your fault, Butch," someone said. "All the press he's gotten has gone to his head and now he's out of control."

Another time, one of Reg's old friends dropped by the office to chat. The man who was older and very distinguished looking kept calling him Reggie. Suddenly, Reg turned on him and declared in a loud voice, "I don't know why you insist on calling me by a childhood nickname. My name is Reg. Other people call me Mr. Lewis. Take your pick."

The man flushed in embarrassment. Chastened, he apologized as the conversation petered out. He finally stood up, made his excuses and left. There was no room in Reg's life for this part of his past.

Reg had changed all right. Around this time, John Baffoe, Reg's chauffeur, drove us to a meeting in Connecticut in the blue Bentley, but wound up getting lost.

"What the fuck is the matter, John?" Reg said. "It looks like you're going in circles."

"I'm sorry, Mr. Lewis," John said. "I think we missed a turn back there."

"Why are you doing this? We're going to be late for our meeting. I don't pay you just to drive. You get my schedule ahead of time. Shouldn't you be studying our route to the next meeting instead of sitting around on your ass all the time? What the fuck!"

Reg slammed his fist against the car door.

"Stop the car!" he shouted.

"What did you say, Mr. Lewis? I think I'll be able to find the way back if you can just leave me alone, sir."

"Stop the fucking car!"

John pulled the car over to the side of the highway. As traffic sped past us, Reg stepped out and opened the door on the driver's side.

"Get out and sit in the back," he told John.

"What do you mean, Mister—"

"Get the fuck out and get in the back of the car."

John unbuckled his seat belt and sat next to me. I watched quietly. What is going on? I thought. Is this supposed to be an elaborate joke? I saw no need to take it this far.

Reg got behind the wheel, took off his jacket and laid it out neatly on the passenger seat. He turned on the motor and started driving with John and me sitting in the back, uncomfortable at this turn of events. Within minutes, he guided us to the venue of our meeting. As we pulled up, we made for an incongruous sight: Reginald F. Lewis, the CEO of TLC Beatrice International, driving his blue Bentley with his Ghanian chauffeur and Filipino PR adviser safely ensconced in the back seat of the car. Reg got out with his jacket, handed the keys back to John and motioned to me to follow him. He said nothing as a smile broke out across his face.

Then in 1989, the same year our public offering failed, our world turned upside down. The government indicted Mike Milken for insider trading, defined as illegally buying or selling stock based on confidential information, and other criminal acts. After a year-long legal battle, Milken agreed to plead guilty to securities and reporting violations and was up for sentencing before a judge in Manhattan. He was a big shot, and the government was determined to make an example of him.

Reg tried to decide whether to write a letter of support for Milken to convince the judge to hand him a lighter sentence. That Mike had helped an African American achieve his entrepreneurial vision counted for a lot, Reg felt.

"What do you think?" Reg asked me from behind his big wooden desk with a sprawling view of Central Park. "Should I?"

"We owe Mike," I said. "That's for sure. But by sending that letter you'd be sticking your neck out and drawing attention to yourself."

"We wouldn't be where we are without Mike."

"That's true."

Reg mulled it over before deciding to write a ten-page heartfelt note to the judge asking for clemency for Mike. I'm not sure if the letter made any difference. In the end, he was sentenced to ten years in prison, a $600 million fine and barred from ever again engaging in the securities business. This was later reduced to two years in consideration of his good behavior and his testimony against some of his fellow defendants. I was proud of Reg for writing that letter. Reg had stood by his friend.

But without Milken, Drexel could not last long. It was forced into bankruptcy in 1990. I had the feeling that the rest of Wall Street, the establishment, did not shed any tears.

Many of the people who worked with Mike went on to bigger things and today are counted among the titans of the business world. He himself walked out of jail and made one of the great comebacks in history, becoming a noted philanthropist. President Trump pardoned him of all offenses, clearing his name. To this day, opinions are sharply divided about Michael Milken.

What I couldn't deny was that without his help, the Beatrice deal would never have happened. Whatever his reasons for backing us, he made a huge difference in our lives. Over the years since he left prison, Mike accomplished a great deal of good with his Milken Family Foundation, pushing the boundaries on a cure for prostate cancer, improving education and many other issues. In any case, the Predators' Ball and the Concorde, along with other curiosities of that era, vanished into the past.

21 — THE BURNING OF BROADVIEW

One day in 1991, we were working in the Paris office when Reg's French secretary, Regine, told us that Lucien, his butler at the Broadview mansion in Amagansett, was calling and that it was urgent.

"What is it, Lucien?" we heard Reg say. "What? . . . How the hell did it happen?" He was screaming now. "Call New York right now and have everyone meet me at Broadview. I want you to stay at the house. DO YOU UNDERSTAND?"

He hung up, ripped the phone from the plug and hurled it against the wall. He was silent for a second, then said ominously, "Butch, tell the pilots we're flying to Long Island right away. Everyone, we're heading for the airport."

He picked up his coat.

"We'll get our clothes at the hotel," I said, "and meet you at the airport, Reg."

"No time for that!" he said. "Broadview's burned down! Forget your clothes. We're leaving for New York with whatever you've got on right now. Regine, call their hotels and have them pack their things and send them to New York."

We were shocked. How could that big old house have burned down? But we had no time to register this information. Reg raced down the stairs to get into the Mercedes and we chased after him.

All through the flight to Long Island, Reg sat pensively by himself in the front cabin making notes on his yellow legal pad and muttering to himself. The rest of us huddled discreetly in the back. There was complete silence. Finally, he called me up front.

As I sat next to him, he showed me what he'd been working on. It was a list of names, and it seemed to include everyone he'd ever known, including many of his oldest and dearest friends. Also on the list was everyone who worked at TLC Group, even the guys in the back of the plane with us. The only name missing was mine. Thank God, I thought with relief.

"Who do you think did it?" Reg asked me "Cleve? Charles? That fucking David? They've all been jealous of me."

When we arrived at Broadview, we pulled up past the entrance leading into the long driveway bordered by waves of green grass. Beyond the tennis court we could see a smoking, blackened hulk, the remains of the grand house. It reminded me of a huge, black vulture that peered down at us, screeching one question: Why? Only the chimney and the concrete garage still stood. Firemen were still running around. Looming over everything hung the thick odor of smoke and ashes. Broadview was one of the landmark houses in the very tony town of Amagansett. Its location, jutting out onto the Atlantic Ocean, was unparalleled. The house had been Reg's refuge from the world, a place where he could relax and be himself. Now all that was gone.

Bimal Amin, our Indian accountant from the New York office, David Guarino, our controller, Kevin Wright, our legal counsel, and I got down on our knees in our suits and dug through what used to be Broadview, though we weren't sure what we were looking for. I couldn't believe that the fancy old house where we'd spent many pleasant hours playing tennis or having barbecues was gone.

The four of us wound up staying there for days, shopping at the nearest department store for our underwear, toothpaste and toothbrushes and anything we needed because everything else was on its way back from Paris.

Reg drifted aimlessly past what was left, his expression impassive. Finally, he spotted a picture frame of the family, showing a smiling Reg, Loida and their two young daughters, Leslie and Christina. He picked it up and carefully brushed off the ashes. "That's something at least," he whispered.

He looked around and scowled at the butler.

"Whatever you do," he said to me, "keep your eye on that fucker over there."

The fire chief approached him. "We got here as fast as we could, Mr. Lewis," he said. "But the fire spread very quickly. The house was mostly wood. By the time we arrived, it was almost gone."

"It doesn't look like you were able to save very much," Reg said. "Any idea on how this thing got started?"

"No, sir," the fire warden said. "Although there doesn't seem to be anything suspicious at this time."

"Nothing unusual? No smell of gasoline?"

"No. But we've got the arson squad going through everything. If there's any evidence of foul play, they'll find it."

"Thank you for your efforts, Chief. Please thank your men for me."

The fire warden nodded and walked off. For a moment, Reg was quiet. "It's almost Thanksgiving," he said to me. "Remind me to send turkeys to all the firehouses that helped along with a note of thanks from me."

His cellphone rang. It was Loida.

"It's bad," he said. "It's pretty much all gone . . . . I know, dear. So many happy memories . . . . No, we're not coming back here. We'll sell the place and move on." He hung up.

Then he kicked into high gear. "Get me the mayor's office," he commanded me. "I want New York City's top arson investigators combing this place. I don't trust these local yokels."

"But Reg," I said, "this is Long Island. The New York City guys don't have any jurisdiction here."

"I don't give a shit. The mayor owes me big time."

I started to walk away when I heard him cry out, "Who do we know at the White House?" Reg and Loida had gone to the White House for big state dinners a couple of times and the Republicans and President George H. W. Bush were courting him for contributions.

"The White House?" I said. "What have they got to do with this?"

"I'm not going to ask you twice," he said, giving me a murderous look. Reginald Lewis still believed that nothing—even the ear of the president of the United States—was beyond his reach.

"We know Andrew Card. He's pretty close to President Bush. He was once his chief of staff and now he's the Transportation Secretary."

"Get him on the car phone." I did as I was told and started explaining the situation to Card when Reg grabbed the phone away from me. "I'll talk to him personally. I'm going to get to the bottom of this no matter what it takes."

Whatever Reg said (and I have no idea whether Andrew Card himself actually did anything), it worked. Not only did New York City's detectives show up, but in a couple of days, so did an Alcohol, Tobacco and Firearms truck. Even I was impressed. Nobody came up with a thing though. When I talked to one of the people from ATF, he gestured, "We're here because some rich Black guy's house burned down."

We even hired our own team out of Boston, who dug through the debris one more time. After a week, they told us that there might be a chance that the fire was deliberately set, but I suspected that they told us this only because they knew it was what Reg wanted to hear. We did, however, get into trouble with the Long Island folks. One of them leaked the story to the New York papers that city resources were being used in an investigation outside the city limits. The headlines were ferocious: "Fire Investigation Angers Long Island Police;" "Brown Defends Sending Officers to Dinkins's L. I. Friend." (Brown was New York's Police Chief Lee Brown.) New York City's finest promptly beat a hasty retreat back to the five boroughs.

We never did find out what happened. Though, looking back, it could have been faulty wiring. The house was old. Or perhaps one of the household staff had partied a little too hard that night. Or maybe, just maybe, some white guys decided to torch the mansion of the only Black man staying in Amagansett. Whatever it was, I was pretty sure that nobody on Reg's list had set fire to Broadview.

22 – THE GRANDEST APARTMENT ON FIFTH AVENUE

Sometime after, Reg's prized blue Bentley was stolen from the parking garage. Suspicion fell on a disgruntled employee who'd been let go and who'd promised him she'd make his life "miserable." Despite the setbacks, Reg came back on stage in 1992 for yet another historic breakthrough. He had always dreamt about living on Fifth Avenue.

"They don't let Blacks live on Fifth," he once told me. "The only ones on the Avenue come in through the servants' entrance. They even turned down Bill Cosby. But I'm going to be the first."

New York co-op boards were notorious for turning people down, no matter who you were or where you came from. The boards were the last bastion of autocracy in America. They never explained the rejections, never gave reasons, never apologized. Once they voted thumbs down, that was it. Some buildings only allowed a certain number of Jews. None entertained even the possibility of selling an apartment to a Black person. Board members and real estate agents said as much in public.

None of that dissuaded Reg. Naturally, he would never settle for just any apartment on Fifth Avenue, either. No, he wanted the best. That meant 834 Fifth Avenue. Residents within that forbidding domain ranged from Laurance Rockefeller and Lee Radziwill (Jackie Kennedy's sister) to David Gutfreund, chairman of Salomon Brothers.

"I'll ask Harold Burson to help," I told Reg. "He knows how to get something like this done."

Harold was the guru of PR. He was a short, balding, courtly Mississippian who started off as a reporter in New York and then decided to cross over to the other side and start his own PR firm. It took him years, but he gradually built it into the largest PR firm in the world. I looked up to him and valued his counsel.

Harold handed me a list of people from whom we had to get letters of reference about Reg to give to the co-op board.

"That's the only way we'll get him into a building like 834," he told me.

It took several weeks but in due time, I finagled letters from some of New York's 500, the elite of society, recommending Reg. What sealed it, or so I heard, was that Rockefeller himself put in a quiet word with the board. When the purchase happened, it shocked the New York City real estate establishment. "The whole real estate world was abuzz in 1992 when Reginald Lewis, the CEO of TLC Beatrice and one of the few Black billionaires of the time (there were no Black billionaires at that time) bought an apartment at 834 Fifth Avenue, perhaps the fanciest building in New York," Frederick Peters wrote in *Forbes* magazine. According to the book, *The Sky's the Limit*, Reg and Loida were two of "the few people of color to own an apartment in a 'Good Building' on Fifth Avenue."

Reg wound up buying the apartment of John DeLorean, the car executive and genius who'd invented the distinctive DeLorean sports car featured in the *Back to the Future* movies. By the time we met DeLorean, his company had gone bankrupt and he'd just escaped federal narcotics charges with a not guilty verdict. He had allegedly sold cocaine to earn enough money to try to save his company, but the jury ruled that he had been entrapped by a federal agent. Now he had no choice but to sell his 15-room, two story apartment with a 640-square-foot living room overlooking Central Park. An apartment with two stories was rare on Fifth Avenue.

We walked into the residence which was spacious and filled with expensive furniture. But it was dark and gloomy, like a cave. It had an Old World, European feel to it. A globe of the world stood sentry in one corner while a large library in dark-paneled wood wrapped itself around one room.

A butler showed us in. DeLorean himself greeted us and briefly showed us around the apartment. He was still distinguished looking with a thick head of gray hair. He slid into an armchair and spoke softly to us. He seemed beaten down by life, not at all the confident CEO and innovator I'd imagined him to be. I could tell from his somewhat downbeat demeanor that he hated selling the place. He sheepishly showed us the drawings for a new electric transportation scheme that he was going to work on with the Japanese. But he was just a shell of the man he used to be. Maybe Scott Fitzgerald was right: "There are no second acts in American lives."

Reg bought the *pied a terre* for $12 million, at the time the highest price ever paid for an apartment in New York City.

Reg threw himself 100% into the project - the massive renovation of his 834 Fifth Avenue apartment. He sought out the foremost designer in New York. One afternoon, he and Loida were looking over their new abode. I tagged along as usual. The doormen were stuffy and welcomed us cautiously. The place was empty and quiet.

"Remind me to send a note to Laurance Rockefeller," Reg told me absent-mindedly. "He was very helpful."

"I love America!" Loida exclaimed.

"Don't get carried away," Reg said to her.

"Where else in the world can people like us move in with the elite? It wasn't that long ago that we had holes in our sofa."

Reg glared at her. "You mean, it wasn't that long ago when I was a successful corporate attorney, don't you?"

She ignored him. "Who's going to decorate it?"

"Just leave all that to me. I've got some famous Argentinian architect to re-do the place. In fact, here he is now."

Just then, a flamboyant and flashily dressed man wandered in.

"Loida, I want you to meet Monsieur Juan Pablo Molyneaux." Ever since Paris, Reg had picked up the habit of calling many foreigners Monsieur.

Molyneaux bowed elaborately and kissed her hand.

"That's Butch over there. He'll be overseeing the whole thing."

That astonished me since I knew absolutely nothing about building or decorating anything, let alone a Fifth Avenue apartment. In fact, I was a pretty clumsy guy. Still, I managed to control the rising sense of panic that gripped me.

"Hi Butch," Molyneaux waved at me with a smile. Then he turned to Reg. "Mr. Lewis, there is no way that I can finish this gigantic makeover in three months. Let me have six."

"Forget it. In fact, let's make it two months."

"Oh, my God!" Molyneaux said. I thought he was going to faint.

"I'll tell you what," Reg said. "Finish the apartment in two months and I'll give you a bonus of $200,000 on top of your fee." Reg grinned and gave me a devilish look.

Molyneaux was speechless, his head hanging down and his mouth open.

"Do we have a deal?" Reg asked me.

"What can I say?" Molyneaux said and threw up his hands as if helpless to resist.

What Reg Lewis wanted, he generally got. He'd lost Broadview but now he was onto a new challenge. He was determined to own the grandest apartment on Fifth Avenue.

Reg pulled me aside.

"There's just one problem with this place."

"What's that?"

"What're all the high-class neighbors going to say when they see all of Loida's friends stop by the building?"

I tried to visualize the scene in my mind.

"Maids' night out," he roared with laughter, and I have to admit that I chuckled even if the joke was a poke at people like me.

Molyneaux threw what seemed like a hundred-man crew into the renovation. He designed a whole new entrance with something like a Roman dome overlooking all who entered. It resembled the entryway to an elaborate mausoleum.

Reg wanted an authentic English library, so he and I flew to London and scoured the furniture shops till he found someone who could do the job. Which was to mobilize a crew of skilled English carpenters, fly them to New York City with their tools, their wood and other material and build an authentic English library. What could be more simple or obvious! He ran me ragged and himself as well. I couldn't believe that we were in London and actually contemplating a plan to fly not just the wood but the workmen to New York City. I mean this was the sort of thing that kings and queens used to do.

The construction proceeded at a frenetic pace. Everyone tripped over each other. Molyneaux screamed in English and Spanish while the Brits were hard at work on the library talking in their distinctive Cockney accents. And who was making his way carefully through the carnage talking on a phone to Paris and reporting on the daily progress? Clueless, not very handy with tools and gadgets, me. My one consolation was that supervising the job meant I could stay in New York and go home at night to my wife like a regular husband.

Reg gave his orders, expected them to be carried out and then jetted off to Paris. He called me daily and I had to faithfully report to him in detail how the painting and the decorating were going. It was like the blind leading the blind, but I did the best I could.

"The color of the living room looks good. That color you picked out, that shade of salmon? It worked out well."

I glanced up at the laborers fumbling on the scaffolds above me. "The ceiling is coming along, too," I lied.

23 – LOOMING STORM

Even as all this panicky activity was taking place, something far more ominous came to pass. I flew off to Paris every now and then to describe to Reg the progress on the apartment in person. During my visits, I noticed that he was beginning to miss days at work. In the past, he had rarely ever missed work. He stayed at home more and I had no clue why.

Loida kept the reason for Reg not showing up for work very hush-hush. Then one day, I overheard two maids gossiping in the Lewis apartment on Palais Bourbon, and tiptoed over to the kitchen to listen in. They were talking in a horrified tone about how difficult it was to clean the bed sheets because there was so much feces on them. Just then, I heard Loida and Reg walking toward the living room. He limped in and struggled to make it to a chair. Loida had to grab him to keep him from falling. I gave them the latest update on the Fifth Avenue construction work. They both listened intently. Neither alluded to anything about his health. Nor did I ask.

Secretly, I worried that Reg was suffering from some kind of disease. He was just 49 and in the prime of life, the height of his success. I was certain he had a long way to go yet. I never thought that the man could be seriously ill. He had been the nexus of my life for six years and I could not imagine what my life would be like if anything happened to him. I returned to New York to focus on the creation of the monument.

Shortly after this episode, Reg and Loida headed back to New York on the jet. The family kept him away from us at the office more and more. Our interaction with him was limited. Previously, Reg had always hung out with the guys at TLC Beatrice a lot more than with his relatives. No one from his family was even allowed to contact the office according to what I assumed were Reg's instructions. His mother, Carolyn Fugett, was a formidable person. She had a personality that made an immediate impression on you. But whenever she called with some request, she would always stress, "Now remember, do not tell my son that I called." She did not want to incur Reg's ire.

Once, Reg and Loida took the plane with other members of the family to Canada to meet some doctors. I heard from the pilots that Reg was loaded onto the plane lying in a cot. A nurse accompanied him. By now, it was clear to me and others that something was seriously wrong with Reg. And that the family was searching for some kind of cure.

One day we learned the answer. Reg was suffering from brain cancer. It was an aggressive form of cancer. We didn't know what to expect. But I knew this much: that if news of his illness leaked to the media, it would alarm the business world and African Americans everywhere. We were a privately held company so we were under no obligation to disclose his illness to the public.

By now, I had come close to quitting my job. But news of his illness shook me. I decided to stay. No matter what, I had this old-fashioned sense of loyalty to him. I guess that's a good way to describe me, old-fashioned, with my reverence for Westerns and playing the hero, and almost preferring to be a good loser instead of winning just to be able to display sportsmanship. This was true even with somebody I didn't like. When I refused to rise to the bait and get into a fight with an opponent, Reg, who liked pitting his boys against one another, would say, "What world did you come from, Butch?" because he couldn't quite fathom why I wouldn't strike back when given the opportunity.

One of my close friends said that my problem was one of stunted development; ethically, I'd never progressed beyond high school, hence my value system. I didn't believe that. I only knew that I should be fair and honest with everyone and that most people were good at heart. My sister Susan told people, "We're the kind of family that would prefer to be fooled than to deliberately fool someone else. We couldn't live with that." That said something for the way we'd been brought up.

24 – "HE GAVE ME HOPE"

Then the moment came when the apartment that Reg had fantasized about for so long was finally ready. By the time Loida and he took possession, he was walking with a cane. That alarmed me because he had always been so vigorous. I wanted to ask him about his illness but chose to keep quiet.

"I got to admit it," Reg said. "That fucker Molyneaux did a great job."

I had to agree. The entrance with the Roman dome overwhelmed guests. The colors of the rooms, salmon, green and dark brown, were warm and cozy. Paintings by French Impressionists, modernists of every nationality and African American artists adorned the walls. The Picasso was striking, as was the Miro and the several Beardens. The apartment looked out at Central Park and the light streamed in, coloring everything in a luminous, almost ghostly light.

All I could think as my gravely ill boss admired the apartment was that maybe it had all come together a little too late.

He and Loida consulted experts on healthy living, who prescribed special diets. Beatrice kept chugging along even without its leader. The staff in New York kept asking about Reg. What's going on? How sick is he? When is he coming back? We've got to make some decisions. They were jumpy. But we were all in the dark, so I didn't know what to tell them.

Loida asked me to fly over a faith healer from the Philippines. I was convinced he was a phony and started to argue. I told her I'd read stories about him and his shenanigans although he did later manage to get elected mayor of Baguio, the mountain retreat north of Manila built by William Howard Taft when he was Governor General of the Philippines.

"Butch, I want him here," Loida said, laying down the law. "He might be able to help."

We flew the so-called faith healer over with three of his friends. They spent most of their time shopping for Gucci bags and designer jeans. I later learned about the "operation," the attempt to "heal" Reg, from some of the family. The man and his team draped a huge blanket over Reg. Then he reached under it to poke around. This went on for almost an hour. Then he suddenly pulled out a mass of bloody tissue. With a flourish, he announced to the family that this was the "cancer" ailing him and pronounced Reg cured.

Later, Reg's brothers, Jean and Tony Fugett, ganged up on me because they held me responsible for the farce. "That guy was a fake," they said. "He just pulled out some pig's insides."

"I knew it was a mistake," I said in my defense. "But we were desperate. Loida thought it was worth a try. And Reg approved it."

Later, Reg told Loida to pay the "faith healer." "It's all right, Loida," Reg told her. "He gave me hope."

25 – THE CURTAIN FALLS

One day, I saw Reg scribbling furiously on his yellow legal pad. It was his autobiography, he told me.

It looked like he'd finished about thirty pages. He showed it to me. Everything was written out in long hand and would be typed up later by either Fay or Norma, our office secretaries.

"That's great, Reg," I said. "Long overdue. It's important to get your story out."

"You know what I'm going to call it?"

"What?"

"Why Should White Guys Have All The Fun?" he said with a laugh.

My jaw dropped in dismay. "But we'll lose the white audience," I said. "It's too 'in your face.'"

"Hell, I don't care."

Reg had previously downplayed his race as a factor in his life, and especially in his success. But here he was finally running up the flag for all to see.

He returned to his writing just then. But he was getting weaker by the day. He tired easily and spent fewer hours at the office. Time was running out for him. I hoped he was a fast writer.

One Saturday, I got a call from Reg. "I want you to get the fuck over here!" he screamed. "This Greek butler has got to go."

We'd retained DeLorean's butler, Stavros, to oversee the Fifth Avenue apartment. I bid a hurried goodbye to Pam, telling her "Reg wants me," and rushed over. The place was dimly lit. By now, Reg's head was swathed in bandages. I didn't ask him what the bandages were for and he didn't offer an explanation. He was leaning on his cane but still exploded with anger.

"I want that fucker out of here!" he screamed. "He got into a fight with the rest of the staff. Time for him to go! You take care of it."

"OK, Reg. I'll handle it."

"And another thing," he said. "I want you to get me on *Larry King*. I want to do an interview." At the time, *Larry King Live* was one of the top talk shows on television.

"You want to go on TV?" I asked. His condition had left him looking less than telegenic but I let that thought go unspoken. Plus, who knew what he was going to say? Would he accuse people of not letting him bid on companies in the U.S.? Might he lose his temper at questions he viewed as impertinent?

In any case, I had my marching orders and told him I'd do what he asked. First, fire the butler. Second, get him on the highest-rated TV talk show in the country. No problem.

Clearly Reg was aching to tell his story to the world one last time. And I was still the guy for the job.

I headed into the kitchen and approached Stavros, a short, distinguished-looking balding older man. He looked concerned.

"I'm sorry," I told him, "but you've got to leave."

"It was those country mice," Stavros said. "They kept doing things the wrong way." He was referring to the butler and the cook who normally stayed at the Amagansett house when there was an Amagansett house. He asked me if I could get Mr. Lewis to reconsider. He was getting older, he said, and it might be hard for him to find a job. I shook my head and said I was sorry. I thanked him for the cheeseburgers he used to buy from a nearby cart to serve to me and the staff, wished him good luck and turned around and left. I felt bad for Stavros but I had other priorities now.

That Monday, I called a producer at CNN's *Larry King Live* show and pitched an interview with Reg. She was cool to the idea.

"What's the angle?" she asked. "What will he talk about?"

I said something about him discussing the TLC Beatrice deal and his next takeover target. I knew Reg hoped to buy the Beatrice operations in the U.S., then still in KKR's portfolio. But they'd held him off from what he believed would be his triumphal comeback.

"They don't want me owning anything in the States! That's the reason they're stalling," he griped.

The Larry King producer remained non-committal. We agreed to resume our discussion.

One day, Reg and Loida were buried in deep discussion. The winter sun shone brightly through the windows, which were double-paned to keep out the cold. The heaters were on full blast, but Reg was bundled up as he slouched on a chair. He shivered. Loida sat close to him, her hand holding tightly to his.

"They're trying to take it away from me, Loida."

"Darling, we can lick this thing."

"It's just that after the failed IPO and the fire at Broadview, for the first time in my life, I don't feel lucky."

"You've got to be optimistic," Loida said. "Believe that you'll recover. Keep a positive attitude. That can make a difference."

"I'm not going to do the chemotherapy," Reg said. "Too destructive. I want my brain to function."

"That might be the only way to keep you alive, my darling. We need to do everything we can to attack this disease."

"I've made up my mind. For Christ's sake, Loida, don't fight me on this one."

"I don't know how to say this, Loida," Reg said. "I don't even know if I should, but ... forgive me."

"For what, darling?"

"For all the times I've hurt you. For all the times I haven't cared."

"Darling, it's OK. We're going to get you well again."

He sat there alone with his thoughts for what seemed a long time. "It's like a shade is falling over my eyes."

Sometime later, I walked quietly into the hallway of 834 Fifth Avenue. I looked out the window and saw couples strolling arm and arm in Central Park. Kids were sledding in the snow. Somewhere a jazz band played a catchy tune. I longed to join them.

I was overcome with deep grief and depression. I had planned to brief Reg on the negotiations with Larry King. But now the situation had worsened and that was off the table. Farewell, I wanted to say to Reg, we had a hell of a run. I turned on my heels and ran out into the cold.

The time came when we heard the news we had expected. Reginald Lewis, age 50, was dead. It was hard for me to believe that a man who was so robust, so ambitious, so full of rage and intensity, was suddenly no more. We'd known each other so well, and I'd served him for so long, done so much together, gone to so many places. He had dominated every day of my life for years. He'd led his team and his company to fight countless battles, persevered through ups and downs, and willed us on to victory. He believed in luck. Yet he also believed in his power to alter his own fate. He had achieved much but he always grasped for more. It was never enough. S*ic transit Gloria mundi*, as the Romans used to say, "thus passes worldly glory."

I was burnt out from all the yelling, but Reg had led us to the Promised Land—9 West 57th Street and Fifth Avenue, the Solow building which sloped down from the top and boasted a huge number 9 at its front. That was Reg's lucky number, 99 Wall Street, 9 West 57th, 9 Rue de la Paix, our Paris office. Whatever he was seeking—dominance, preeminence, peace—eluded him, lost in the storm of life, in the challenge of race and the ceaseless pushing and striving of a man.

I called Pam to tell her the news and she said she would stop by the church to pray for Reg. I called my father and let him know what had happened. He felt bad that someone who had everything could die so young. The women in our Paris office, whom Reg had always treated better than the New York crew—every morning cheerily greeting them with *"Bonjour!"*—broke down in tears on hearing about his death. The guys in New York were stunned. I was caught in a fog, unclear about what the future held for me, Pam, or for any of the thousands of people at TLC Beatrice International.

The day Reg died, Loida invited a couple of us to the hospital and ushered us in to show us his body. The room itself was bare and tiny and looked like a morgue. Reg lay there on what appeared to be a concrete slab, wrapped in a white hospital robe, his head turned slightly sideways. All the anger, all the drive and all the dreams were gone. We just stood there staring at what was left of him, a shape, a form, a mere memory. So, this is how it ends. This is what awaits all of us. Rich or poor, powerful or powerless, it's all the same. We are all going to die. I was going to die, not perhaps that day or the next but someday. I too would lie silent and still with whatever it was that made me Butch Meily whisked away, to what I did not know.

After a few minutes to say privately whatever prayers we could muster, we moved to another room to talk about plans for his wake. The first was to be held in Baltimore and the second in New York City at the fashionable Riverside Church on the West Side.

"Reg once told me that if he ever went, he'd like a simple, classy service like Lloyd Garrison's," I said. Garrison was a well-respected New York lawyer whose wake Reg and I had attended. It consisted of a few readings from the

Bible and brief responses from the family and someone from his law firm.

I was so used to telling people what Reg wanted and having everyone fall into line without question that I was taken aback when Loida balked. "Reg is dead," she said, "I'm in charge now."

"I'd like a service with Jesse Jackson, Mayor Dinkins, Arthur Ashe and others speaking," she added. The few senior executives from TLC who were present looked at her, shocked and silent. Who was this person? But just like that, I knew the answer. We had a new voice at the table, one from whom we had never heard.

At a later meeting, the company executives met with members of the Lewis family to discuss the communications plan. The family wanted to ease the shock of his death by first announcing that Reg was sick and then saying that he passed away. No one outside this tight group even knew that he was ill. But this was a big story, impossible to hide. I believed that we should have a press conference to tell everyone the news. But the family was adamant. They wanted first his sickness and then subsequently his death declared with just a simple statement. For some reason, they wanted to keep everything under wraps. I knew this was a mistake. It went against everything I believed in about public relations. You've got to tell the truth and if it's bad news, it's best to get it out quickly. But I was lost and in unchartered waters. Reg had just passed away. In the end, I went along with it.

We agreed that I'd put out two press releases, the first saying Reg was ill and in a coma, and then a second, a few hours later, announcing he had passed away.

I sat down in my office and looked out at Central Park which was covered in white, taking time to search for the figures of people trudging through the snow. Then I composed two of the strangest press releases of my life. After the first release went out, I started getting calls from Reg's close friends. One lady insisted he'd recover and be just as good as before.

"I don't think so," I answered. She burst into tears and accused me of being pessimistic and giving up prematurely. It seemed useless for me to explain. I felt bad about lying to people, pretending that Reg was still alive when I knew all along that he was already dead. Here I was, managing the image of a dead man as if he were still alive.

As soon as the second release crossed the wires, all hell broke loose. The *Larry King* producer called five or six times. CBS and NBC reached out too.

The message slips piled up on my desk. Everyone wanted to know what had happened. The media staked out various New York City hospitals to find out where his body was. The story in the *Los Angeles Times* that went out at 12 a.m. Pacific time on January 20, 1993 read:

Reginald F. Lewis, the Harvard-educated lawyer who gained fame during the 1980s takeover craze and built the nation's largest black-owned business, died of a cerebral hemorrhage Tuesday after a short battle with brain cancer. The quick decline of the chairman and chief executive of TLC Beatrice International Holdings, who turned 50 last month, came as a shock to Lewis' friends and colleagues. Many learned of the extent of his illness Monday, when the multinational food company revealed that Lewis had been hospitalized in Manhattan and was in a coma . . . . At the request of Lewis' family, the company released no other details about his illness, including the name of the hospital where he died.

For one last time, Reginald Lewis was front-page news.

26 - A SECOND BLOW

Baltimore was dreary and overcast as our train lumbered into the station. It was so chilly the morning of January 23 that I remember putting on my long underwear, my coat and tie, my heavy overcoat, my hat and my gloves and sticking my hands into my pockets, but I was still cold. I had to stamp my feet on the icy ground to keep warm.

I was in charge of the larger wake in New York, but the funeral in Baltimore was the family's affair. Pam came along with me as well as all the guys in the New York office. It was an impressive service. One by one, various luminaries spoke. Baltimore Mayor Kurt Schmoke, the Archbishop of Baltimore, the Reverend Ben Chavis, several TLC Beatrice board members. Sam Peabody, one of the original investors in the McCall Pattern deal and a TLC Beatrice board member, read from a poem, John Masefield's "Life Is Eternal":

A ship at my side spreads her white sails to the morning breeze and starts for the blue ocean....'There, she's gone.'...Gone from my sight... there are other eyes watching her coming, and other voices ... shout, 'There, she comes.

Loida's words were especially meaningful:

"I have loved you without conditions. I have loved you without reservations, and my love for you will never end... And I shall see you again when it is my time to be with you."

Then-President Bill Clinton, former President Ronald Reagan, Colin Powell, Henry Kravis of KKR, the governor of Virginia and the head of the NAACP all sent condolence messages. The European managers flew in. Even the Bauds were solemn and respectful. We listened to the tributes. Then we were all given a chance to pay our respects before the coffin and take one last glimpse of the man who'd been the center of our universe for so long.

As I stood up, I heard one of the guys whisper, "The only reason I'm going up there is to make sure that SOB is dead."

A few of us served as pallbearers along with Reg's family and we gingerly carried the coffin out of the church and into the cemetery at its back. As we lay the coffin down, I saw that a crowd had gathered. I noticed a motorcycle cop eying me. He started trooping towards me, then dropped off to speak in whispers to the chief pilot of the TLC Beatrice jet, Brendan Flannery. Brendan nodded at him and then approached me cautiously. He pulled me aside.

"Butch, I've got some bad news for you. That officer said that your brother in law from Iowa called." I waited anxiously. Pam sidled up to me and grabbed my arm.

Then Brendan breathed a sigh as he murmured, "Your father died last night in Manila."

I stared at him uncomprehendingly. I asked him to repeat what he'd said. Then I reached out to Pam, who started to cry, and I staggered. I couldn't understand it. I had planned to call my father the night before to have one of our regular chats and tell him about Reg's wake. But because I was so busy, I'd put it off.

I felt God was trying to tell me something. He'd taken away Reg and now my father within four days. Was His message that it was time for me to stand on my own? My father, just a long-distance phone call away if I needed support and suggestions, had always encouraged and advised me. "His father idolized Butch," Pam later said. He had been my rock. Now, at age 73, he was gone. I'd have given anything for a few more minutes to talk to him and get his words of wisdom one last time.

I thanked Brendan and held on tightly to Pam. I knew what I had to do. I marched to Loida and the rest of the family to tell them that my father had died. I had to fly home to Manila right away and would be unable to supervise the wake in New York. Loida readily agreed and told me to take the jet back to New York.

I'd set up most of the preparations for the wake already anyway and I now contacted Chris Atkins, my former boss at Burson, to oversee everything. I had previously called in the Burson New York team to handle all the calls from the press and the public that were flooding in. I'd even called Arthur Ashe, the famed Black tennis star, to ask him to speak at the wake in New York. "Sure, Butch," he readily agreed. Little did I realize that he himself would be dead of AIDS which he had contracted through a blood transfusion within two weeks.

The rest of the month was a blur. The journey back home for Pam and me was long but I was caught up in my memories of my father. America changed me. I wasn't the same person as when I'd gotten on that plane in 1977. I was no longer the shy nerd that I used to be. I was much more confident now. The States had given me that.

Once we arrived in Manila, I helped my mother, brother and four sisters to make all the arrangements necessary to lay my father to rest. I had a checklist of things to do. I placed a bereavement ad in the papers. Wrote a press release. Paid the taxes. Sorted out my father's advertising business. Settled any debts and then sold the company. I wanted to ensure that Mom had the funds to live the rest of her life with dignity.

Later I learned how my father died. He and Mom had been giving a talk to an audience of college girls. Afterwards, they walked down some steps and he crumpled to the floor with a cry. A heart attack or an aneurysm, the doctors said. My mother said he looked as if he was already dead. She turned her eyes to the sky and cried, "God, is that all there is?" Married 42 years and all she wanted was to keep it going.

Hundreds of people flocked to my father's funeral. He was laid out in his Knights of St. Sylvester uniform complete with cap and sword. (St. Sylvester was a papal order of knighthood meant to honor Catholic lay persons who had performed great service to the Church.) I delivered the eulogy. Everything I said came from the heart. I talked about our years together and the years apart, about how I loved and admired him, and how he'd taught me how to someday be a good father. The Cardinal, who was his close friend, presided over the Mass and spoke as well. A group of mourners approached me about petitioning the Pope to name my father a saint. I politely put them off.

I later discovered his diary with pages and pages of what he experienced when he was courting my mother. They burst open with the kind of wild passionate love that only the very young feel. "I was panting and happy—choking. Held her hand and kissed it so many times. I am really down and out for her." Dad was young once too and in love.

I wondered what my life would have been like if I hadn't left. I could have had more time with them. Years later, I came to understand how precious that time together as a family was. But sometimes you have to say goodbye to those you love if you are to find your path in life. It was hard for me to imagine returning to the country for good. When I met my old classmates, they appeared to have stayed the same, the same jokes and playful taunts. It was as if we'd never left school. The problem was that I had changed and experienced so much of the world while everything else seemed frozen in time.

Staying in my old room, I understood the emotional cost my parents had paid for my absence. My room was like a shrine with all my medals and certificates from school carefully preserved. Coming home every day to an empty house once teeming with life and filled with memories must have been depressing for my parents. No wonder they had thrown themselves into those trips around the country, giving talks to groups of every kind about marriage and family life. For three years, they served as the President Couple of the Christian Family Movement, the largest family organization in the country at the time and my father, who was a marketing man at heart, made sure stories about their talks appeared regularly in the papers. At least, they'd built a new life for themselves after we left.

"Those years visiting all of you in the States were the best times for us," Mom told me.

But to her credit, my mother picked herself up and persevered. She decided to soldier on, carrying on their weekly column at the national magazine, *Panorama*, and retitled it from "Husband and Wife Speak" to "And Life Goes On." I think she was the better writer (sorry, Dad!) and her columns carried more depth and less Church dogma. She covered topics such as "Boredom in Marriage," "A Confused Husband," and "Sex in Old Age." Her column continued to be one of the most popular in the country, according to reader surveys.

27 – THE WAKE

I took more time to clean up Dad's affairs and make sure my mother was all right and then, a little reluctantly, flew back to New York. When I got there, I learned about the wake at Riverside Church on the Upper West Side of the city which lasted hours. There were many speeches and some songs.

The Harlem Boys Choir, one of Reg's charities, sang as did the opera singer, Kathleen Battle, and Filipina Broadway star Lea Salonga. Loida and her daughters, Leslie and Christina, spoke, as they had at the Baltimore service. The Reverend Jesse Jackson, Percy Sutton, the Manhattan borough chief, Kevin Wright, TLC Beatrice's General Counsel, the CEO of Texaco and the Dean of Harvard Law School all eulogized him.

The Reverend Ben Chavis acknowledged Reg as the chief counsel for the Commission for Racial Justice of the United Church of Christ during the battle to free the Wilmington Ten, a battle they eventually won. Reg "used his legal training … and his unique ability to formulate effective strategies in assisting us in the civil rights movement."

Vincent O'Sullivan, the head of Tayto, TLC Beatrice's potato chips company in Ireland, said Reg "was equally at home reviewing supermarkets in Paris, ice cream in Denmark, soft drinks in Holland, or yogurt in the Canary Islands."

New York City Mayor David Dinkins declared that "Reginald Lewis accomplished more in a half century than most of us could ever deem imaginable." His life proved "to us all, and especially to African Americans, that dreams deferred need not dry up like 'a raisin in the sun.'"

The Reverend Al Sharpton, a future presidential candidate like Jesse Jackson, sat quietly in a back pew. I was sorry that I missed the service. I would have wanted to say a few words.

I still had some unfinished business burnishing the Reg Lewis legend. He had donated $3 million to Harvard Law School, then its largest individual donation ever. The International Law Building was renamed the Reginald F. Lewis International Law Center in his honor, the first building on the Harvard campus named after an African-American.

Its inauguration in April 1993 was a standing-room-only affair. Even the crusader Ralph Nader stood respectfully in the back of the hall.

Leslie Lewis quoted from F. Scott Fitzgerald's unfinished final novel, *The Last Tycoon*:

"He had flown so high to see, on strong wings, when he was young... he had stayed up there from his great height...but this was where he had come to earth after that extraordinary illuminating flight where he saw which way we were going, and how we looked doing it, and how much of it mattered."

Then we all trooped outside where the family pulled down a canvas to unveil the new name of the building.

Loida persuaded the board of the Harvard Club in New York, the site of so many of our business meetings, to hang his portrait on its walls. At the time, it was the only portrait of an African American there. Even in death, Reg was still breaking barriers.

My life had changed, and I felt different now. The cornerstone around which I'd painstakingly constructed my existence—Reginald Lewis—had crumbled. And my father, my closest confidant and adviser, was gone too. Burned by both losses, I felt my self-assurance draining away.

"You used to be so confident, Butch," Pam said to me. I sensed she was beginning to lose respect for me, and that hurt. I would call her several times a day to ask her advice about petty office matters.

"C'mon, Butch," she'd complain angrily, "you don't need to call me all the time. Make a decision." We were growing farther apart. The gap had been there all along but I had been too blind to notice. I felt that she wanted a husband she could look up to and admire, and I was no longer that person.

I took long walks in Central Park to try to figure out my new life. What was it really all about? Why did we work so hard if only to wind up on a slab in the hospital? For money? Could money buy us extra time with the people we loved? Would money bring back my father?

28 – WE'VE DECIDED TO STREAMLINE COSTS

With Reg's departure, the company plunged into a period of transition and turmoil. Because I was at the center of the company and Reg's guy, I couldn't avoid getting swept up in it in ways I never expected.

The job of CEO of TLC Beatrice International fell to his brother, Jean Fugett. Growing up, Jean was the star and Reg, although older, played second fiddle. Jean had played college football at Amherst, then went on to play tight end for both the Dallas Cowboys and the Washington Redskins in the National Football League. He won a Super Bowl ring with the Cowboys and was named to the NFL's Pro Bowl team while with the Redskins. To his credit, he took night classes while a pro football player and earned a law degree from George Washington University. Eventually Reg became the star of the family and Jean went to work for him at Beatrice. Now Jean took over as my boss. Reg was a hard act to follow and people were always comparing them. It must have been tough for Jean.

I viewed this next chapter of my life with trepidation. Reg had dominated the company for so long. I didn't know what to expect and I wasn't sure how to play the game. In corporate life, there is always an agenda, a set of rules, centers of power that revolve around the CEO that you have to recognize and adapt to. If you are left out or shoved aside, you will not be around for very long.

Jean and I had known each other for some time. He differed from Reg in so many ways, more easy-going and fun-loving, a burly giant surprisingly gentle for an NFL veteran. Now he moved into Reg's old office—it seemed strange seeing him there —and the tension that once contaminated the office evaporated.

"Hey, man, I'm just trying to have as much fun as I can before one of you guys figures out that I don't know what I'm doing," Jean would chortle, characteristically self-effacing.

I had less of a relationship with Jean than I had with Reg, and for someone in my position, that spelled trouble. New CEOs usually want to install their own public relations advisers. Without Reg around, I felt like I had lost my compass. But still I went through the motions of doing my job faithfully.

One day, Jean made a momentous decision. He called us all into his office and told us TLC Beatrice International would bid for the Baltimore Orioles baseball team, now up for sale.

"Butch, you could run public relations for the Orioles," Jean said with a grin. "I know you like baseball. Wouldn't that be a great job?"

Yes, I thought, that would be an extraordinary experience. I asked Jean if we had the financing for the bid and he said he had it.

Peter Angelos, a Baltimore lawyer who'd made a fortune in class action suits, led one of the competing groups. He offered Jean a percentage if he joined them. Jean turned him down. He believed that a minority position in the team would be unacceptable for the leading African American entrepreneur which he now apparently considered himself to be.

In short order, an army of TLC Beatrice lawyers and accountants paraded into a crowded Manhattan courtroom where the auction for the Baltimore Orioles would take place. The judge turned to them now and then to see if they would participate, but they sat through the whole process silent as sphinxes. In the end, Angelos' group won the bid.

The media quickly turned against us for leading a European food company in a failed effort to acquire an American baseball team. For our shareholders, already skeptical about an ex-football player becoming CEO of the company, the misadventure was the last straw. It eventually led TLC Beatrice to a huge change in course.

One day Jean called me into his office. Sitting next to him was our new corporate counsel and David, our controller. As though for the first time, I noticed the elegant French wall clock that Reg had purchased in Paris and the lush Lebanese carpet adorned with peacocks beneath our feet.

The lawyer did all the talking.

"Butch," the lawyer said, "we've decided to streamline costs at Beatrice. It wasn't an easy decision for Jean because you've been part of the company for so long. But we've decided that it might be best if you went out on your own."

I looked at Jean. His eyes were fixed on the floor. I'd never been fired before. But I was only mildly surprised. I knew I didn't quite fit in with the new order of things. I never achieved as close a connection with Jean as I had with Reg. In fact, I never tried. I only rarely joined Jean on his trips to Paris or to the European operations and made no effort to joke around with him.

"We'll give you a severance package, of course, subject to your signing a few agreements," the lawyer said, droning on.

I stared at the carpet, lost in trying to figure out what I was going to do. How would I tell Pam? I acted as nonchalantly as I could. I wanted to deprive them of taking any satisfaction in my unceremonious departure, a pattern I adopted during personal crises throughout my life.

"Thanks," I said, and hurried out of the office.

I entered the Manhattan building where Pam and I lived, wondering if we could still afford to stay there. "Hello, Mr. Meily! How was your day?" our doorman yelled out. I nodded at him, rode the elevator upstairs and unlocked the door to our apartment. Funny, what you remember about such moments. Pam had on a dress with a pattern of colored flowers and was sitting on a rattan chair from the Philippines reading a magazine. I looked at her for an instant. Then I spat out the news. She looked at me silently and then burst into tears. I pulled her close to me.

"We'll be all right," I told her, though I felt no such assurance. We had saved up the money from my bonuses but that would not last if nothing was coming in. It was a daunting prospect to face the fact that my stream of income had dried up. "I'm getting a severance check from the company. It'll tide us over for a while. I've always wanted to start my own PR agency, so I guess now is as good a time as any to start."

I was scared. I could tell she was, too.

"But are we going to make it?" Pam asked.

"Don't worry. We'll be OK."

Pam kept sobbing and I held her tightly.

For the first time in a long while, I was jobless, except now I had a wife to worry about.

29 – THE COUP

Now I was out on my own and had to hustle for business. I was no longer protected by a job in the comfortable confines of a prestigious corporate post. We tried to cut expenses where we could. I picked up one or two clients, but nowhere near enough to make up for my lost income. Bills piled up. The uncertainty we faced was unsettling.

Then one day, the telephone rang. It was Loida's assistant. She asked me to meet Loida at the restaurant of the Plaza Athenee hotel on 64th Street after dinner that night. I didn't know what to expect but meeting Loida was always a pleasant experience. As I walked in, I spotted her sitting at a table. Next to her was her sister, Mely Nicolas. Mely had been Special Assistant to one Philippine president and a Cabinet Secretary to a second. I sat down next to them. Then with a smile on her face, Loida proceeded to tell me about her plan to take over the leadership of TLC Beatrice International. I stared at her with surprise but with growing anticipation. The board and the shareholders were unhappy with the direction of the company—in particular, with the abortive bid to buy the Baltimore Orioles. It made no strategic sense for a European food company to acquire an American sports franchise.

She was bringing in a new leadership team. She wanted me to come back to head the company's public relations department, the same role that I'd played under Reg. When I went home that night, I pulled Pam close to me to tell her the news. We hugged each other happily.

In 1994, one year after taking over the company, Jean resigned. It was announced that Loida Nicolas Lewis, the widow of Reginald Lewis, would become chairman of TLC Beatrice International on February 1 and "that a search had begun for a new CEO." Jean was to remain as a member of TLC Beatrice's board and management committee.

"Ex-CEO's Brother Out, Widow in at Beatrice," bluntly proclaimed the *Tampa Bay Times*.

Looking back, the story did have elements of melodrama and even Shakespeare. I was content to be part of it, on the winning side, and to have my old job back.

The Beatrice offices still looked the same, but I felt different being there now. Nothing could disguise the reality that I'd been booted out and then magically reappeared. Everyone said hello, welcome back. They most likely recognized that because I was close to Loida, they'd better treat me carefully.

Loida quickly established as her first order of business that, as leaders go, she would be almost nothing like her husband.

"Let us begin the meeting by putting ourselves in the presence of the Lord," she told the senior management of TLC Beatrice assembled in a conference room one day. Executives rolled their eyes.

My public relations challenge was to establish her credibility with the business community. She was a new, untested leader of a multi-billion-dollar, multinational firm. Loida's assumption of leadership was greeted by widespread derision on Wall Street. Even her own executives harbored doubts. And who could blame them? Loida's only experience was as an immigration attorney and a corporate wife. The prevailing sentiment was that a housewife had taken over TLC Beatrice. But the Lewis family controlled the majority of the shares. Reg had seen to that. Most of the board were family friends of long standing. Drexel and the other shareholders went along with the change for now. They probably expected a short stay for Loida before she sold the company and they could cash in. What mattered to me was that I was back in my element, seeking to create the recipe that would produce positive press, and grateful to once again savor the good life. I knew which side I was on. I was on board for the ride for however long it would last.

In the end, the search for a new CEO was quietly abandoned. Once she was in charge, Loida had no intention of ceding power. She acted decisively to right the ship. She moved rapidly to communicate that she was her own person and that she knew what she was doing. First, she downsized the New York corporate staff by fifty percent. In doing so, she let go of many of the old guard and installed her own team of advisers. Second, she moved us out of one of the swankiest addresses in New York City to mere cubicles in much more modest surroundings a few blocks away. Third, she sold our beloved corporate jet, now viewed as a symbol of everything wrong at the company. The life that we knew and reveled in was gone with the wind.

Clearly, Loida had studied the Beatrice operations while she lived in Paris and paid close attention to Reg when he talked about the business. Clearly, she had her own hopes and skills. But she had suppressed any ambitions she might have harbored all these years to preserve her marriage to a domineering personality in whose shadow she was forced to live. Finally free to express herself, no longer relegated to the sidelines, Loida blossomed. Her mantra was simple: cut costs, repay debt, and increase earnings.

And it worked. TLC Beatrice's annual revenues in 1994 of $1.82 billion made it the heftiest of any female-run company.

Shareholders liked what Loida was doing. So did women, the Filipino community, and other minorities. Both Coretta Scott King, Martin Luther King's widow, and Mrs. Rachel Robinson, Jackie Robinson's widow, stopped by to visit her a few times because they now viewed her as a fellow pioneer and female leader. "Hi Butch," they'd greet me.

"New Most Powerful Female Executive Is Anointed ... Loida Lewis of TLC Beatrice Has Assumed the Mantle," announced the *Los Angeles Times* in April 1995.

"Top Female Executive Rescued Family Business," said the *Tampa Bay Times* that same month.

Working Woman magazine put her on its May 1995 cover and named her the most powerful female executive in the country.

Performance before publicity, that was a credo Reg had drummed into me, and I abided by it now. And so began the process of rebuilding the myth that was TLC Beatrice International.

Loida was able to smooth our relationships with our European managers, including the Bauds and the prickly Sanson. Maybe because she'd suffered so much under Reg or maybe because it came naturally to her, she was determined to be a kinder, gentler leader. She was a nurturer, a listener, and a consoler. To be honest, she filled us all with love, a very different feeling from what her husband gave us. The speeches I wrote for her expressed her compassionate, caring nature. She always wanted to end with a quote from one of the prophets in the Bible. And there lay the foundation on which everything else in her life rested: her unwavering belief in a good, merciful, wise God who, no matter what, would always be there for us.

But make no mistake: she could be tough when she had to be.

One time, Loida and I met in Paris with Jean and Jacques Baud to negotiate over a new warehouse. "No, Jean," she said with a smile, "we will not give you ownership of the warehouse that we built. That's not going to happen."

"But Madame Lewis," he pleaded, "we believe that warehouse should be part of our business."

"It is part of the business," she agreed, "but the ownership stays with Beatrice. After all, we built it. Do you have anything else that you would like to discuss, Monsieur?"

The two brothers looked at each other, stumped. And that was that. The warehouse would stay with Beatrice.

I always left Loida's office feeling upbeat and optimistic, no matter how dejected my mood going in. It was amazing. I enjoyed working for her and she made me feel good about myself. Yes, she was right. Everything would turn out well in the end. Just trust in the Lord. I still hang on to that belief to this day.

The press adored her. The concept of a corporate spouse taking over and running the company "just like I run my home"—as she put it—was irresistible.

"Mrs. Lewis Proves Her Critics Wrong," declared the *International Herald Tribune* in April 1996. In an interview from Loida's "Paris pied-a-terre," the reporter, Max Berley, wrote:

Her claims to being 'just a wife' have to be taken with a grain of salt. ... In the two years since she became head of TLC Beatrice, she has stepped out of the shadow of her charismatic husband and has become a power in her own right, winning bitter boardroom battles and restructuring the company....

And then came our message, *To restore order to her husband's creation, Mrs. Lewis immediately began a massive restructuring. She sold the corporate jet, got rid of noncore assets, slashed the headquarters staff by half, and hired a new chief financial officer. Her plan worked, and the doubters who thought that a woman with no business experience and lacking a business school degree was not up to the task of pulling a major company out of the red were proved wrong.*

Game over. We had won. Full stop.

"Butch, you've made me bigger than life," she said.

But that really wasn't true. Loida Nicolas Lewis had done it all by herself.

30 – A BEGINNING AND AN END

With Loida as CEO, we all got to take more time off to be with our families. It was a novel experience. Pam and I would spend weekends in our upstate New York country home in the town of Woodstock. I never hesitated to tell Loida where I'd be, whereas with Reg I had tried to hide and escape from him as much as possible. I'd never even told Reg about the Woodstock house since buying it in 1992. The house stood high up on a mountain in the Catskills and featured huge picture windows that wrapped around the house and invited the surrounding forest in. When we woke up, it felt like we were part of the woods. We could listen to the birds chirping, instead of the garbage trucks in the city. It was my refuge, my hideaway from all my troubles at work.

Pam and I turned our attention to having children. She was 33. And she had matured. It was no longer all about me. The relationship had evolved to one on a more equal footing. She knew what she wanted.

"Butch, we need to start a family," she said. "My clock is ticking."

Having children was harder than I expected. Twice, Pam had miscarriages. The doctors concluded that Pam had to have complete bed rest for the entire time she was carrying a baby if this was going to work.

Pam became pregnant yet again. It was the winter of 1996, a year after Derek Jeter joined the Yankees and three years after the deaths of both Reg and my Dad. Manhattan was shut down by a blizzard. People used skis to get around the city. One evening, Pam and I found ourselves threading our way carefully through the snow to get to New York University Hospital on First Avenue and East 34th St. Her labor pains had started. It was the middle of the night and we'd failed to find cabs or anything else that was running. She was hurting and all I could do was hold on to her and make sure she didn't slip. The pain had worsened by the time we reached the hospital.

She demanded the doctor give her an epidural, an anesthetic injected directly into the spine. "I want it," she screamed at the nurses, banging her fist on the wall. "I want it!"

Eventually, the doctor agreed. The epidural calmed her down within minutes. She spent hours in labor, and then we finally possessed what we had at first put off but now wanted more than anything else in the world. Pam gave birth to a son. We decided to name him Marco because Pam said she liked the idea of him being like Marco Polo, bringing East and West together.

And just like that, my life changed forever. All at once I felt a profound love for this new person in our family, and an equally profound sense of responsibility to care for him. I'd never had the time when I was working with Reg to even consider a family.

"If you'd have had Marco while you were still working with Reg," Loida told me, "something would have had to give."

She was right. In fact, if I'd have had a child back then, I probably would have quit. Reg wanted everything from you, leaving you no room for anything —or anyone—else. Now I knew better. Now, if I had to choose, I would choose family over career.

Why Should White Guys Have All The Fun?

At TLC Beatrice, Loida set about further preserving Reg's legacy. She hired a writer, *Baltimore Sun* business reporter Blair Walker, to turn the autobiography Reg had started into a biography. My job was to help Blair, who had never met Reg, to get to know him—who he was as a person—and to experience his life and understand what he had accomplished. I accompanied him on a tour of the TLC Beatrice plants where he interviewed all the managers. He spoke to members of the Lewis family as well.

One day Blair asked me, "What would Reg think of me writing this book? How would we have gotten along?"

After a short pause, I decided to give him an honest answer. "He probably would have fired you," I said. "Then he would have gone through a series of other writers before finally doing it himself. He was a perfectionist, and this book would have been an important project for him. It would have been hell."

Then Blair asked me an even harder question.

"He wasn't a nice guy, was he?"

Again, I hesitated, struggling to find a balance between my still intact loyalty to Reg and my inclination to tell Blair the truth. But I was his PR person. It was my job to keep the legend alive. Then again, it felt creepy to keep polishing the image of a dead man. I'd never revealed even to Loida the truth of everything that I had witnessed.

Finally, I came up with an answer.

"You'll pick up what kind of person he was from the interviews," I said. "Let's just say that he had a lot of pressure on him. Some of it he put on himself. He felt that he was representing all Black people anytime that he tried for something. It was an extra burden that he carried."

In time, Blair created a portrait of the man and his life, at least the version that we wanted to show the world. This is what Reg would have wanted, I told myself. We kept Reg's original title for the book, *Why Should White Guys Have All The Fun?* We added the subtitle *How Reginald Lewis Created A Billion-Dollar Empire.*

Loida promoted the book, published by John Wiley in 1995, with all her heart. She refused to rest until we'd done everything we could to sell it. Charlie Rose interviewed her on his PBS talk show. Neil Cavuto had her over on Fox Business News. He later called his talk with her one of the best interviews he'd ever done. The *New York Post* ran a big spread. Lines formed in front of Black bookstores nationwide. It seemed to be a catharsis for her. I joined Loida, Blair and Carolyn Fugett, Reg's mother, for two cross-country book tours. I saw to it that the PR machine to showcase Reginald Lewis kept running long after his death, all of us co-conspirators in presenting a Reg Lewis who existed partly in myth.

During one of our tours, I suggested to Loida that since she was still relatively young, she should remarry. It was a stupid question and I should have known the answer.

"Get married again?" she yelled in disbelief. "No way!"

Years later, talking with Loida about Reg, I learned the reason why, a reason I should have guessed all along.

"Love never dies," she said.

The Lawsuit

Meanwhile, Carlton Investments, a partnership that included many of the former Drexel executives, sued us for Reg's compensation and expenses, which they believed to be excessive and against the interests of the shareholders. "Ex-Drexel Officials Still Feud with Lewis, Despite his Death," reported *The Wall Street Journal.* From his prison cell, Milken put as much distance as he could from the lawsuit. "Milken Distances Himself from Lawsuit Attacking TLC Beatrice," said the Associated Press.

We were all deposed in a Delaware courtroom. I answered questions from the witness chair in a courtroom that was empty except for the lawyers and a stenographer recording my every word. The opposing attorney asked me a question about Reginald Lewis that no one had ever asked me before.

"Were you and he friends?" she asked.

I paused for a long time before answering.

"I'm not sure if we thought of ourselves as friends," I said. "I worked for him. I was his employee. Reg would confide in me and we spent a great deal of time together. But I'm not sure if, in an employer-employee relationship, you could ever see your boss as a friend."

Were we friends? Or was he just my boss and I one of his faithful employees? Whatever the case, he had certainly trusted me. Late at night, talking either at the office in Paris or New York or in a bistro sipping champagne over dinner, Reg would confide in me about his dreams and plans for the future.

The litigation dragged on, and, after a while, Loida decided to settle, because, as she put it, "The only people getting rich here are the lawyers."

Either way, it was apparent that the Drexel boys were disgruntled and wanted to cash out of the deal. It was as though they resented that we were still around and TLC Beatrice International wasn't put to bed and its assets sold off.

Loida thrived at being CEO and running the company. In 1996, our revenues had reached a high of $2.2 billion. We argued fiercely about the future of TLC Beatrice. The former Drexel group, owner of 26 percent of the company, wanted to sell it. Most of the management team wanted to keep it intact and thereby hold on to their jobs.

"Loida, if you sell the company, you won't be CEO of anything," a Beatrice executive told her. "It won't be the same. You won't get the same respect as you do now."

But none of that mattered to her.

In the end, Loida made what I believe was one of the most difficult decisions of her life. Without Reg around to push back against Drexel, it was hard for us to hold the line. The phrase we kept hearing was shareholder value, never mind the consumers and the employees. We had to listen to Drexel and others when it came to major decisions. Loida sold off the last pieces of the empire. The ice cream companies, the Irish potato chip maker, our French supermarkets—all were auctioned off one by one. "TLC Beatrice to Sell

Remaining Divisions," ran the headline in *The New York Times* in May, 1999. Our time in the sun was ending just as the old century drew to a close.

"Reg may have launched the ship and steered it," Harold Burson would tell me years later, "but Loida is the one who brought it home."

Goodbye to 834

The next thing Loida did was get rid of Reg's 834 Fifth Avenue apartment, the monument that I helped erect. She was all by herself and she wasn't planning to remarry, so two stories on Fifth was a bit much for one lady. She sold the edifice that we'd labored on and that had made its way into New York real estate history as the first Black-owned apartment on Fifth Avenue. She moved into a smaller, tasteful, cheery apartment that was still on Fifth Avenue and still overlooked Central Park, only this time it stared out over the reservoir. Displayed in the new apartment was all of the artwork along with a case of Reg's belongings: his old eyeglasses, cigar cutter, photos.

With the company sold, we had to close up the shop. It was time for all of us to say goodbye to life as we knew it and move on to new lives. I had spent eleven years, much of my working life, at TLC Beatrice. So much had changed; I'd gotten married, become a father and lost both my father and my boss. I felt transported to a different world.

Reg had lifted me and others to a whole new tier financially. He also raised the level of my game professionally. No matter how good I might be at my job, because he was so demanding, he made me better. He did that with everyone. With the sale, I felt like the show was over. None of us would have an easy time adjusting to a new life, least of all me. Nothing I would go on to professionally would ever come close to being as exciting as those years at Beatrice with Reg and Loida, or so I thought.

A small group stayed behind to unwind the taxes on all those companies, but most of us left. I turned over the press kits, the video tapes, the sheaf of news clippings. I could picture Reg smiling in one of those iconic photographs taken by famed photographer Gregory Heisler. There was the one of Reg posing in a green trench coat on the Pont Alexandre in Paris, very much in the style of Humphrey Bogart. There was the second photo of him smiling, leaning against the door in his Manhattan office, impeccably dressed in a suit with a pocket square while he casually held on to a pair of glasses, one of his artworks poking its head in the background. Then there was the shot of him smiling confidently at the camera while dressed in a suit, sitting on his desk, arms across his lap with the Empire State building and the rest of the Manhattan skyline framed behind him in a blue light. We'd worked so hard to get those photos. They weren't easy shoots because of Reg's explosive temperament but they'd been worth it, capturing him at his best for posterity. I stuffed a few mementos into my briefcase, bade adieu to everyone who'd been part of my life for so long, took the elevator down and walked out into the tumult of the city.

31 – LOSS AND REDEMPTION

I searched for a job, connecting with friends and headhunters. I flew to job interviews in Beaverton, Oregon; Chattanooga, Tennessee; Omaha, Nebraska and lots of places in between. Pam understood that we might have to move for the job. In the end, I decided to return to what I knew best, the PR agency business in New York City, this time with Rubenstein Associates, a well-known firm. There, I advised clients, cranked out press releases and every Friday afternoon listed my media "hits" for the week. I worked in the business and financial PR unit led by Peter Rosenthal, an experienced and hard-nosed PR practitioner.

One advantage was that I was able to take time to be with the family, and that was a blessing. We moved to Stamford, Connecticut to give Marco, Pam and me more room. Christmastime, the three of us along with Marco's friends, would spend the night looking for Rudolph's nose. After a time, we'd spot a plane's flashing lights and triumphantly proclaim it as Santa's sleigh with Rudolph in the lead. Then we'd rush to the yard and build a snowman.

Every night before Marco fell asleep, he made me tell him the story of the movie, *A Bug's Life*. It didn't matter how often I told it, he just had to hear it. Sometimes I told it to him straight. Other times I varied my voice to mimic the characters at which he'd giggle. Years later, he said to me, "I remember your telling me those stories, Dad. It never got old." Our son had a pleasant disposition and the confident smile of someone who knew he was loved.

Later I took him to New York Knicks and New York Yankees games, echoing a family tradition going back to my father and I staying up late at night in Manila to listen to the World Series on the radio.

"Thanks, Dad!" Marco blurted out to me excitedly once. "I wish we could stay like this forever."

"You're going to grow older sooner or later."

"Of course, I am. But that doesn't mean that things have to change."

Yet I knew from my life with Reg that things always change. I knew that you can seemingly have it all and die at 50. The little boy before me who liked watching black-and-white movies with me was going to grow up and move on.

Manila

I eventually decided to take a job working with one of the highest profile tycoons in the Philippines, Manny Pangilinan. He'd ventured overseas at a young age, just like me, although his destination had been Hong Kong. While there, he'd built a firm of six people into a Southeast Asian investment power-house and was now pouring huge amounts of money into the Philippines. He bought everything: the phone company, the water company, the power company, a big mining firm, a large road-building entity, a slew of hospitals. To me, this was the Asian version of Reg and Beatrice International. I was back in the saddle again. I hoped to recapture the glamor and the meaningfulness of my time with Reg.

I started out writing this book to show people the richness of characters that I'd known and worked with over the years and to reveal the insights that I'd drawn from them about life. What I hadn't intended was to write about a relationship, a marriage. But no career stands alone, isolated from the rest of the world. It's always connected to a web of relationships, or the lack of them, husband to wife, father to son.

Marco texted me at work— "Come home, Dad, so we can go on vacation." Maybe that was really from Pam.

I'd spent much of my married life away from her, in Europe with Reg, and now the same thing was happening with Manny. I worked while Pam stayed home and took care of things. What was different in Manila was that we had a lot more leisure time since someone else was doing the cooking and the cleaning. None of that mattered, though, because my working hours were brutal. We often stayed in the office until 2 am and worked on weekends too. I felt like I was chained to a desk at work. I should have paid attention earlier. But things were changing quickly between Pam and me. She wasn't the young girl I'd taken to Central Park on that first date.

My return to Manila and my work at the top of the business world did not save my marriage. In time, Pam and I drifted apart.

The day came when she told me that she wanted her own place. And I acquiesced.

I never imagined this would happen to me. Divorce was something that happened to other people. I'd built my life around her and had imagined us growing old together. Our meeting at that Fourth of July party at Sutton Place seemed predestined. Why else would God have thrown two random souls together?

I lost what perhaps I should have valued most and had taken for granted. I promised myself that if I was ever in a relationship again, I would stay home more and be more attentive and caring. This isn't exactly how I thought things would turn out when I started out in New York City so full of dreams and ambition. The wife of Jean Pierre, my old colleague from Paris days, once told me that life is like a walk in the park. Some people join you for part of the walk and then step aside even as others jump alongside you. My mother, who is 92 now, answered me when I asked her why my marriage had soured, "It wasn't meant to be, Butch." Yes, Mom, you're right. Some things aren't meant to be.

With my marriage gone, one of the anchors of my life drifted away. I had nothing left in the tank. Then God threw me a lifeline.

Manny made me head of the company's charitable foundation. At first, I viewed it as a chore. I eventually recognized it as a chance at redemption. It gave me the opportunity to bounce back from my failed marriage and reinvent myself in my new role as a humanitarian. I would make our corporate social responsibility function about more than just handing out checks.

As my first project, I picked one that was close to home and would help people I saw every day. I established a microfinance loan program for the company's waiters, janitors and security guards. They weren't regular employees and frequently had to surrender their earnings to pay back moneylenders who charged exorbitant interest rates. My program rescued them from that morass.

I finally found something that made me feel good at the end of the day. Someone's life improved because I happened to be alive and was around to give them a hand. I had no clue though that I would be in the pilot's seat at a time when the country was about to careen through a slew of calamities.

Every year, some twenty or more typhoons slam into the Philippines. Our family's most vivid memory was seeing Dad, a World War II veteran, scrambling down the steps from the second floor of the house screaming in fear as the wind ripped the roof off. But the storm that curled its way towards the central part of the archipelago in November 2013 was a beast out of hell. It was a typhoon called Haiyan and one of the most powerful cyclones ever to make land. As it approached the islands, it attained winds of up to 195 miles per hour.

No one knew what to expect. Many of the people in the city of Tacloban where the storm was headed paid it no attention. They had been through typhoons before and this one was no different. Others took the warnings to heart and fled. On such decisions turned the fate of thousands. Those who left survived. Many of those who stayed perished. What people didn't expect were the huge storm surges with water rising up to 17 feet that swept away everything in its path in the early morning hours of November 7. Families who had moved to a school that had been designated as an evacuation site were trapped in a classroom and drowned there.

Philippine Air Force responders who were gearing up to help at the airport terminal which sat on the edge of a bay found themselves caught up in a deluge. Some were only able to escape after clawing their way through the roof with their bare hands. The commander was discovered alive bobbing in the water in his life vest miles away from the airport. Even the mayor's family barely escaped with their lives when they were trapped at their beach house.

From 6,000 to 10,000 people died. Many of the bodies floated out to sea and for months, city residents refused to eat fish for fear that they might be consuming one of their neighbors. Bodies were still being discovered in January 2014. I managed to fly into the city by helicopter a few days after the typhoon struck. As we hovered closer, I saw steel towers coiled up as though a giant had wrapped them around each other, testifying to the force of the winds.

We landed in a sports stadium. I spotted two government officials amidst a troop of soldiers who were resting. They were busy texting. When one of them recognized me, he asked me what I was doing there. Was I a tourist? he smirked.

I pointed at my cap with the name of our foundation. We wanted to help, I explained.

"We don't need you," he proclaimed. "I've got mountains of relief goods at the airport. Now that you're here, why don't you go outside? Get a feel for it." He said it with a sneer.

Feeling challenged, I jumped into a car and drove outside.

What I saw stunned me. Crowds of starving people trying to get food trailed relief trucks. Dead bodies lay under galvanized steel sheets. I spotted a sign on the road asking to have thirty bodies picked up. People stopped ambulances to ask their crews to pick up the dead but were waved off. They had to concentrate on rescuing the living.

It was clear that this was one of the seminal events of our time and we had to respond. After a previous typhoon, the president of the Philippines had asked Manny to lead recovery efforts and he put me in charge. My foundation morphed into the Philippine Disaster Resilience Foundation (PDRF), made up of many of the largest corporations in the country. It transformed my life. Up to this time, I'd worked for CEOs but had never really run an organization. I had to keep reminding myself to report to the board because I was so used to just popping in to tell Reg or Manny what I planned to do and getting their approval. I also felt the weight of being responsible for the livelihood of dozens of individuals. A lot of people depended on me and my judgment.

We received a flood of donations locally and from overseas and I busied myself rebuilding health clinics and classrooms and helping revive small businesses. We constructed evacuation centers where the community could run to when the next typhoon struck. It brought tears to my eyes to see the kids smile, sing songs of welcome and wave their handmade paper flags of gratitude. When I was asked to speak a year later at the graduation of one of the schools that was hardest hit by the storm and where I knew many of the survivors would be in the audience, I could only muster the words of the 23rd Psalm: "The Lord is my Shepherd; I shall not want . . . Yea, though I walk through the valley of the shadow of death, I will fear no evil . . ."

I spoke haltingly because I knew that no matter what I said, it wouldn't be enough to compensate for the audience's pain and suffering. I met a teacher, Geraldine Marasigan, who lost her grip on her six-year-old daughter and watched her float out into the ocean. I spoke to Prinz, an 11-year-old whose four sisters died in the storm.

"Sir, thank you for coming to Tacloban," Geraldine said as she held on tightly to my hand. "We're so grateful."

"That's OK, ma'am," I told her. "You're the real heroes, not us."

I moved to take a photo of Prinz but someone with more sense warned me off. He'd suffered enough.

I felt a commitment and a compassion for the victims of the typhoon that filled me with a love that had been missing from my life for years. I felt that this was my moment. Whereas before I was glorifying individuals like the

Flying Viking, the Jamaican Prime Minister and Reg Lewis, now I was lifting people up, giving them an opportunity to put their lives back together. This was the port that I had been sailing for all along. I was changing people's lives, making things better. Maybe I wasn't happy at home, but I was helping others and that brings its own fulfillment.

Haiyan was a catastrophe, but it raised the profile of our foundation as we became an important player in the global humanitarian preparedness, response, and recovery effort. I felt proud of the work we were doing and of everything that we had accomplished. We managed to show the world that the private sector had a role to play in managing disasters. More importantly, we'd helped hundreds of thousands of people with our programs.

Our foundation did so well that we received an award from an organization in London and I met then-Prince Charles, who told me, "The problem with the Philippines is that it's in the wrong place. It gets hit by all these typhoons."

Yes, I agreed. If we could tow the whole archipelago to somewhere else like Norway, we would do it.

Through PDRF, we had created something new—the private sector as a force for good in a world filled with catastrophes. The UN flew me to Fiji, Vietnam, Sri Lanka and Panama to help establish similar business disaster management networks. I traveled to Istanbul for the World Humanitarian Summit in 2016. There they launched the Connecting Business Initiative, a global network of businesses modeled on PDRF. I spoke at the closing ceremonies before a thousand people. I ended with a quote from Dag Hammarskjöld, the UN's first Secretary General who died in a mysterious plane crash while trying to negotiate a peace settlement in a civil war in the Congo. I suspect that it came as a surprise to these humanitarians that someone from the business community would quote their hero:

"I don't know Who or what put the question. I don't know when it was put. I don't even remember answering. But at some moment, I answered 'Yes' to Someone or Something and from that hour I was certain that existence is meaningful and that my life had a goal."

EPILOGUE

These days, I focus on my work at the foundation. At night, I lay down in my bed, turn up the air-conditioner really high and put a blanket over me. Sometimes as I lay awake at night, I think back to those days with Curtis Hoxter, the Jamaican Prime Minister, and Reginald Lewis. They are all dead now but they still inhabit my life like shimmery ghosts. Late at night, my mind helplessly wanders back to those days in New York, which at the time seemed so real and the most important thing in the world, but now live only in my mind.

Recently, Marco texted me from Los Angeles, where he now lives. "Don't worry about all that stuff, Dad. There were so many fruitful and amazing times that I don't think you should look at it with such disdain. And there are many more amazing moments still to come. I am 100% certain of that."

That was one good thing at least that I'd had a hand in, I tell myself. He has ambitions of being a writer, sort of taking after his father, I like to think.

From where I am sitting, I can glance out the window and if it's the right time of day, I can watch the sun setting on Manila Bay, bathing the horizon with an orange light, radiant and glorious. It looks like a slice of heaven. I remember Reg Lewis' anthem, keep going, no matter what. Then I pick myself up and tell myself that I'm not quite done yet; there are one or two more campaigns that I can mount and perhaps save the world.

After prolonged contact with individuals in power, I've concluded that living an average life, with a loving family and being able to do what you want during your spare time leads to far more happiness in the long run. High positions and even wealth are overrated. Ordinary living and loving are better.

As for myself, I really do need to finish that book that I started writing in the last century while sitting alone in the New York Public Library, before the end. I have many times over the years started to put pen to paper, then stopped, halted by inertia or a lack of time or a deficiency of imagination. I realize now that it's the story of my life and that if I can write that last page, some part of it will endure, so that, if nothing else, Marco will understand who I was and how I lived and what it was all about.

SCENE LIST

The following is a list of the scenes to which I refer in my Author Notes:

☐ Chapter 5: Description of the meeting at TLC Group: I depicted this scene based on interviews with key participants and my own recollections and impressions. I combined various discrete discussions into one scene for narrative purposes.

☐ Chapter 7: Meeting between Reginald Lewis and Michael Milken and Peter Ackerman: This scene conflates different meetings and discussions that took place including two meetings at Drexel's office in Beverly Hills in June 1987. I created this scene based on my conversations with Reginald Lewis, the Walker book and my understanding of the characters and the nature of discussions and negotiations. I folded Drexel's demand for equity in the Beatrice International deal and other talks including several on the phone into this one meeting for dramatic purposes.

☐ Chapter 8: Discussion between Reginald and Loida Lewis and myself: This scene is based on my recollections of several conversations with Reginald Lewis. I combined those conversations into one scene for narrative purposes.

☐ Chapter 10-11: The Beatrice auction: I created these scenes based on interviews with several participants, my recollections of my conversations with Reginald Lewis at the time, the Walker book and my impressions of the characters involved. I combined the auction for Beatrice International and the closing of the transaction into one evening for dramatic purposes.

☐ Chapter 10: Scene with the Australian buyers: I created this scene based on my recollections of my conversations with Reginald Lewis at the time, the Walker biography and my understanding of the character of Reginald Lewis.

☐ Chapter 14: Discussion between Reginald Lewis and Cleve Christophe: This scene is based on my interview with Cleve Christophe.

☐ Chapters 17 and 25: Discussions between Reginald Lewis and Loida Lewis: I created these scenes based on the Walker book, my recollections of Reginald and Loida Lewis, and conversations with Reginald Lewis and with Loida Lewis over the years.

ACKNOWLEDGMENTS

I want to thank Loida N. Lewis for her unstinting support of the book along with the many editors who at one time or another worked on the manuscript — from Grub Street, Caroline Leavitt, Maria Mutch, Ethan Gilsdorf, Sara Freeman, my former Rubenstein PR colleague, Bob Brody, Kelly Branchal and my final editor Jeff Ourvan. My gratitude also goes to my lawyer, Jessica Friedman, who combed through the manuscript many times, my publisher, Naomi Rosenblatt, for having the faith to print it, my niece, Cecile Aranez who designed the book's cover, and my former wife, Pam, who lived much of this story with me. My thanks as well to my former TLC Beatrice colleagues particularly Charles Clarkson, Cleve Christophe and Jean Pierre Tegnet who helped me immensely and to the many others who I wasn't able to mention in the book but who nevertheless played important roles in the saga that was TLC Beatrice International. And of course, let me acknowledge Reginald F. Lewis for being such an extraordinary individual and courageous leader.

AUTHOR BIO

Butch Meily has lived much of his life shuttling between the U.S. and the Philippines. He served as Vice President, Communications for TLC Beatrice International, a food company in New York and Paris, for 11 years. He worked for several New York public relations firms and a financial startup there.

Currently, Butch is President of Philippine Disaster Resilience Foundation, a private sector disaster management organization that includes major business groups and won global recognition for its work. He also heads IdeaSpace, a technology accelerator for early-stage startups, and QBO Innovation Hub, a public private sector partnership to mentor startups.

Butch has written articles for the *Wall Street Journal, Chicago Tribune, New York Daily News, Baltimore Sun, Black Enterprise* magazine, the *Philippine Star* and RealClearMarkets.com.

Butch holds an M.A. from University of Florida, receiving its Most Distinguished Alumnus award in 2000 and becoming Freedom Forum Distinguished Visiting Professor in 2003 and a member of the College of Journalism and Communication's Hall of Fame. Butch is a graduate of Ateneo De Manila University.

www.ingramcontent.com/pod-product-compliance
Lightning Source LLC
Chambersburg PA
CBHW030940150426
42812CB00064B/3086/J